Globalization
and the Kingdom of God

The Kuyper Lecture Series

The annual Kuyper Lecture is presented by the Center for Public Justice in cooperation with leading institutions throughout the country. The lecture seeks to enlarge public understanding of three dynamics at work in the world today: the driving influence of competing religions in public life, the comprehensive claims of Jesus Christ on the world, and the strength of the Christian community's international bonds. The lecture is named in honor of Abraham Kuyper (1837–1920), a leading Dutch Christian statesman, theologian, educator, and journalist.

The Center for Public Justice is an independent, nonprofit organization that conducts public policy research and pursues civic education programs, such as the Kuyper Lecture, from the standpoint of a comprehensive Christian worldview. The Center's purpose is to serve God, advance justice, and transform public life. It carries out its mission by equipping citizens, developing leaders, and shaping policy.

Each book in the Kuyper Lecture series presents an annual Kuyper Lecture together with the responses given to it.

Books in the Kuyper Lecture Series

Mark A. Noll, *Adding Cross to Crown: The Political Significance of Christ's Passion,* with responses by James D. Bratt, Max L. Stackhouse, and James W. Skillen (the 1995 lecture).

Calvin B. DeWitt, *Caring for Creation: Responsible Stewardship of God's Handiwork,* with responses by Richard A. Baer Jr., Thomas Sieger Derr, and Vernon J. Ehlers (the 1996 lecture).

Dan Coats, *Mending Fences: Renewing Justice between Government and Civil Society,* with responses by Glenn C. Loury, Mary Nelson, and Stanley W. Carlson-Thies (the 1997 lecture).

Elizabeth Fox-Genovese, *Women and the Future of the Family,* with responses by Stanley J. Grenz, Mardi Keyes, and Mary Stewart Van Leeuwen (the 1998 lecture).

Bob Goudzwaard, *Globalization and the Kingdom of God,* with responses by Brian Fikkert, Larry Reed, and Adolfo García de la Sienra (the 1999 lecture).

The Center for Public Justice
P.O. Box 48368
Washington, D.C. 20002
410-571-6300
www.cpjustice.org

Globalization
and the Kingdom of God

BOB GOUDZWAARD

with responses by

Brian Fikkert

Larry Reed

Adolfo García de la Sienra

edited by James W. Skillen

P.O. Box 48368
Washington, D.C. 20002

A Division of Baker Book House Co
Grand Rapids, Michigan 49516

© 2001 by The Center for Public Justice

Published by Baker Books
a division of Baker Book House Company
P.O. Box 6287, Grand Rapids, MI 49516-6287

Printed in the United States of America

Library of Congress Cataloging-in-Publication Data

Goudzwaard, B.
    Globalization and the Kingdom of God / Bob Goudzwaard ; with responses by Brian Fikkert, Larry Reed, Adolfo García de la Sienra ; edited by James W. Skillen.
        p.   cm.—(The Kuyper lecture series)
    Includes bibliographical references.
    ISBN 0-8010-6354-X (paper)
    1. Globalization—Religious aspects—Christianity. 2. Church and social problems. I. Fikkert, Brian. II. Reed, Larry. III. García de la Sienra, Adolfo. IV. Skillen, James W. V. Title. VI. Series.
JZ1318.G678   2001
303.48'2—dc21   00-046829

For current information about all releases from Baker Book House, visit our web site:
                    http://www.bakerbooks.com

Contents

Foreword

James W. Skillen

Globalization will increasingly characterize the twenty-first century. What is globalization? In brief, it features the growing interdependence of people throughout the world. Interdependency is multiplying and intensifying by means of ever more rapid means of communication, which are helping to tie the world's billions of still multiplying people closer and closer together economically, environmentally, technologically, and in other ways. Globalization also means a change of perspective on the meaning of life. As Bob Goudzwaard explains in his 1999 Kuyper Lecture, the globe has itself become a platform for action, a point of departure and not just a destination. Right before our eyes, on the Internet, on TV, on the labels of products we buy, and in the

James W. Skillen (Ph.D., Duke University) is president of the Center for Public Justice. Previously he taught politics at Messiah, Gordon, and Dordt colleges. He is the author of several works, including *The Scattered Voice: Christians at Odds in the Public Square* (Grand Rapids: Zondervan, 1990) and *Recharging the American Experiment: Principled Pluralism for Genuine Civic Community* (Grand Rapids: Baker, 1994).

people we meet, we see humanity exercising dominion over the whole earth—in a single "global village."

The village of humanity, however, is more and more characterized by extremes of wealth and poverty, of optimism and hopelessness, at least economically speaking. This picture is captured in a few sentences by Alan Cowell, who traveled to central Africa just after leaving Davos, Switzerland, where leaders of the richest nations and largest corporations gather annually for the World Economic Forum.

> In Davos, according to one survey, 50 percent of business leaders thought the Internet-driven New Economy would help close the gap between rich and poor, and 38 percent thought it would not. Those figures seemed surreal in places like Jimbe on the Zambia-Angola border, 50 miles of dirt track from the nearest telephone or electric power. When conversation in Switzerland turned to "the market," the word denoted global tides of trillions of dollars flowing through the wired world. At Jimbe, "the market" meant a twice-weekly sale of scrawny chickens and plump pineapples, which had been suspended since Angola launched a bombing attack a few months earlier.
>
> The question, in a place like Jimbe, is not so much whether globalization would help the poor in these parts of the developing world, as whether it extended here at all. Globalization, after all, unites those with the training and resources to leap onto a speeding technological bandwagon. But what of those condemned, often by their own leaders' greed and incompetence as much as by anything else, to the roadside?[1]

Globalization should not surprise Christians, who confess that God created one world and sent forth the first man and woman to populate and steward the entire earth. Nor are Christians shocked by the fact that much of the populating and "stewarding" has amounted to destruction, oppression, and unspeakable poverty. From Adam and Eve's first disobedience has sprung a history of multigenerational disobedience to the Creator, who entrusted us with so much. Christians may not wallow or lose hope in the darkness, for their very identity is marked by repentance, thanksgiving, and hope. God did not discard or depart from the creation so misused and fouled by the men and women who fill it and are supposed to steward it wisely. In Christ Jesus, God became human in order to reconcile and redeem the world— the whole earth. The reconciling work of Christ is as all-encompassing as humanity's fall into sin, so that not one inch of creation is left untouched. Yet that good news of redemption, restoration, and reconciliation calls Christians to confront and address the reality of poverty and degradation around the world.

The burden of Bob Goudzwaard's 1999 Kuyper Lecture is to shed light on the religiously deep wellsprings of contemporary economic globalization. He begins by assessing some of the most evident developments in today's international economy and then digs deeper into the institutional or structural framework that undergirds those developments. Finally, he arrives at the deepest level, where he sees people—especially westerners—hypnotized by acquisitiveness and competition, fearful of falling behind or not getting ahead fast enough, acting like children who believe there is no other way to "make progress," even though poverty and environmental degradation grow worse rather than better. Like prophets of old, Goudzwaard calls for the fearful to wake up, to shake off their hypnosis in order to become "mature, realistic, and open-faced" human beings once again. And this means accepting responsibility, by God's redeeming grace, for the bad economic decisions they are making and for the malformed institutions they have passively accepted or helped create. Globalization can take a better rather than a worse direction if we learn obedience to the Creator-Redeemer of the ends of the earth.

Goudzwaard has been dealing with these questions and working on these issues for a long time, first as a student of economics, then as a member of the Dutch Parliament, then as a university professor and adviser to business, labor, and political leaders, and now as a participant in numerous international organizations and conferences—of churches, universities, think tanks, and economic institutions. The respondents to Goudzwaard's Kuyper Lecture are younger Christians, equally concerned about the future of the global economy and about human responsibility and irresponsibility.

Brian Fikkert, who teaches economics at Covenant College, asks whether Goudzwaard has adequately weighed the biblical teaching about the "already" and the "not yet" of God's kingdom. Since sin is still so prevalent, don't we have to work at establishing institutions and making economic decisions in that light? The best international economic arrangements may be those that take for granted the self-interest of peoples and nations, not those that try to establish an unreachable ideal of global justice. Moreover, it is not just the West's competitiveness and lust for more and more goods and services that are at fault for the poverty of people in the less-developed parts of the world. Poorer countries and regions have their own sinful cultures and institutions. If not everyone around the world is awakening from a dangerous hypnosis, how should that affect the way Christians act economically? One of the most important things Western Christians can do, says Fikkert, is to take a holistic approach to poverty. One way to do that is to promote microenterprise development in conjunction with other means of physical and spiritual service to those in need. Microenterprise development makes small loans available to poor people, who otherwise would not have access to capital, empowering them to overcome poverty and dependency.

Larry Reed works full-time with Opportunity International, an international microenterprise developer. He agrees with Goudzwaard's analysis of the religious-root crisis of Western-led globalization and stresses that Christians are far too much a part of the darkness rather than part of the light. Christians probably control $10 trillion around the globe, or about one-quarter of the world's annual production of wealth. If they were to decide to invest their wealth differently and shape institutions differently, they could change the global economy. In addition to microenterprise development, Reed offers other suggestions for action to individuals, families, employees, churches, and international organizations.

Finally, Adolfo García de la Sienra, a Mexican economist/philosopher, accepts Goudzwaard's wake-up call as a challenge to professional economists. Just as global economic trends seem to be powered, in many ways, by a spirit of disobedience to the Creator-Redeemer, so economic theory is generally grounded in humanistic assumptions of a mechanistic and evolutionistic character. Christians must work with different assumptions, which should lead to a different kind of economic theory that can give a better account of reality and better guidance to wise economic development.

In the conclusion, I draw together some of the threads from the Kuyper Lecture and the three responses to begin charting a course for the public policy work of the Center for Public Justice and other organizations whose members want to act globally on the basis of a biblical vision of life, in thankful response to the Giver and Redeemer of life.

1

The Spirit of Our Age

"Our nineteenth century is dying away under the hypnosis of the dogma of Evolution." With these words, Abraham Kuyper opened his presidential address at the Free University of Amsterdam on October 20, 1899.[1] Tonight, on October 28, 1999, we meet on the eve of a new millennium as well as a new century. How shall we characterize the world's spiritual and cultural climate at the close of the twentieth century? Under what kind of hypnosis might we be living?

These are very difficult questions, and it would be all too easy for us to try to evade them. Yet Christians have a responsibility to live in close touch with our societies, to understand the signs of the times, and to discern the spirit—or spirits—of the age. That responsibility becomes greater at key moments of historical transition. We are about to cross the bridge into a new century, and we must face squarely the biblical truth that, as a historian once said, "Every generation stands directly before the face of God." We may not merely lean on the shoulders of past generations and past leaders—even important Christian leaders such as Abraham Kuyper.

Trying to answer questions about the spirit of our age may seem like an impossible task. Our society and the world have become so enormously complex, much more so than a century ago, and Christians hold diverse views of reality. Any attempt to interpret the signs of our times must, therefore, be undertaken with great care and humility, starting with a clear-eyed assessment of the concrete circumstances in which we find ourselves.

Kuyper started with the firm assumption that the dogma of evolution dominated Western society as a new and integrating worldview. "Until now in our Christian circles," he said, "we had the inspiration of a faith that bound all things into a unity, giving us an advantage over our opponents. . . . But due to the dogma of evolution, non-Christians, too, now possess an all-encompassing system, a world- and life-view derived from a single principle, a new found Monism."[2] The root of evolutionary monism, as Kuyper saw it, is to be found in the mechanistic assumptions of the Enlightenment. The idea of an evolutionary "unfolding" process is *organic,* but it is controlled by a dogma that "tolerates nothing but *mechanistic* action from the beginning to the end."[3]

On the basis of this religiously deep insight, Kuyper then proceeded to interpret the social reality around him, linking the atheistic dogma of evolution to the social, economic, and political dynamics of his time. The depth-level control of evolutionary dogma, he believed, helped explain, for instance, why stronger nations try "to put an end to the lower-level existence of nations which are smaller and therefore weaker."[4] It also helped explain the materialistic tendencies, the eagerness for sensual pleasures, the passion for money-power, and the violent passion for economic expansion.[5]

How Should We Assess the Spirit of Our Age?

Given the complexity of our own age, with its multiplicity of idols and spirits, it may be better for us to follow the reverse order: To assess the spirits and dogmas of our time, we should perhaps first give careful attention to the multiplicity of factual processes. Bernard Zylstra taught us to move from this level to the social order and its structural formations, and then to go deeper, via the underlying layer of culture, to religious drives.[6] In his view, every society, however much controlled by false dogmas, is embedded in the structure of God's creation that constantly calls for human response, for a human answer to God's call. Thus, an assessment of any social process or development can and should be finally based on a judgment about its openness or closedness, its obedience or disobedience, to the liberating message of God's kingdom.

Two additional preliminary remarks are necessary. First, the main frontier in the development of human society today is undoubtedly the international arena, particularly the economic and technological dimensions of that arena. There, usually under the title "globalization," we find the most rapid movements and changes with the heaviest social and political impacts. We must give careful consideration to these global developments if we are to understand the spirit of our era.

The second remark is to caution against giving too much weight to our first intuitive impressions, for in most cases they lack the necessary precision. For example, Harvey Cox stated recently that in our time "the Market is becoming more like Yahweh of the Old Testament—not just our superior deity, but . . . the only true God whose reign must now be universally accepted and who allows for no rivals," an "omnipotent, omnipresent and omniscient God."[7] This may sound impressive and even contain elements of truth, but if other authors say almost the same thing about modern technology,[8] or about the power of money, or about transnational corporations as the new rulers of the world,[9] or about the idolatrous quest for world government, then we should realize that greater accuracy is needed in making these kinds of judgments.

The International Arena

Turning our attention to the leading factual processes of our day, we are struck by the fact that within a period of only ten or twenty years, a host of new words has entered the media and filled public debate. Think of *networking, database, transnational corporations, globalization, information society, advertorials,* and *edutainment.* Yet even more striking is the fact that all of these new words have had an international dimension right from the start. Obviously the globe has become more than simply a *possible* horizon for human actions; it now serves as a platform from which actions spring.

New transnational corporations (TNCs), for example, transcend the borders of the national state right from their inception. They are, so to speak, born to be footloose, meant to act globally from the outset. At the same time, however, the TNCs are gaining enormous power and market strength inside particular countries, dispersing their commercials to family rooms all over the world. Something similar is happening in the financial sector, especially in regard to short-term international capital flows. These flows are also global from the beginning and are therefore correctly called movements of "global capital," for, just like a satellite, they circle the earth without a tie to a specific country. That kind of capital can leave your country within days or minutes if elsewhere a fractionally higher financial reward is expected.

Changes in the economic and financial sector have been enormous, but they would have remained unimaginable apart from worldwide technological advances. Due to breakthroughs in information technology, financial transactions can now be made within fractions of a second all around the world. Global networking has become part of daily life. The expanding Internet is now a common feature of business and, increasingly, even a family asset. The globe has become an added layer of human consciousness, especially for our net-surfing and video-playing children. *Time* magazine (3 February 1997) wrote a few years ago of the planetary awakening of humankind.

This awakening is also related to new production methods such as bioengineering. Industries adopt technological changes more rapidly than ever before, and the changes are patented worldwide from the outset. More and more economists are now convinced that these changes are producing a "new economics."[10] Productivity is increasing around the world, especially in technologically advanced countries. This entails risks of overinvestment, as evidenced in the recent Asian crisis. Yet the new economics is also characterized by the simultaneous appearance of lower interest rates, lower unemployment, and pressure for greater consumer demand, for to absorb the enormous increase in global productivity, global expenditures must grow.

In the "Network Economy,"[11] we face what Carl Shapiro and Hal Varian describe as the inversion of the law of supply and demand. Production costs of information technology continue to go down even as the demand for equipment and software goes up. This is leading to the practice of near "zero pricing." Bill Gates installed Windows Explorer at no charge in order to eliminate Netscape as a possible competitor. Thus, in the field of information technology, abundance seems to be permanently eliminating scarcity, but at the cost to the consumer of being "locked in" by the suppliers.

2

An Assessment of Globalization

How shall we evaluate the rapidly spiraling changes in technology, finance, and economic practice that are deeply and broadly influencing our societies and making people very insecure?

As in the Middle Ages, so today we are hearing many predictions of economic and social collapse and even of the end of the world—the final judgment. Many who condemn the entire process of globalization as a demonic endeavor leading people to the abyss also thereby find an alibi to excuse themselves from any responsibility for what is taking place.[1] Let me say emphatically that those who stand in Calvin's line may not adopt this attitude. I decry it and have three arguments for doing so.

A Christian Perspective on Globalization

The first is that the Christian church—the body of Christ—was, from the start, also meant to become a global community. While some of Jesus' disciples wanted to restrict the gospel message to the Jewish people, the Holy

Spirit made it clear that all nations of the world should hear the Good News and participate in the new life. Thus, long before the present process of technological and economic globalization began, God's message of global Good News went forth and began its work. The idea of globalization, therefore, is not foreign to the Bible. In fact, Paul uses a Greek word that is very close in meaning to "globalization." In his letter to the Ephesians, Paul writes about the last mystery that God is unveiling, namely, "to bring all things in heaven and on earth together under one head, even Christ" (1:10). God is guiding or administering the course of history toward that end. The Greek word for *administration*, which is used here, has the same root as the word *economy*. Thus, we might say that God's economy entails its own style of globalization, oriented to the coming of his Messiah King. The question, then, is not whether Christians should be for or against globalization. Instead, the question is, "What kind of globalization should we be supporting?"

My second argument has to do with the "fullness" of life, as that word is used, for example, in the psalms. "The earth is the LORD's and the *fulness* thereof" (Ps. 24:1 KJV, emphasis added). Scientific results, technological breakthroughs, and worldwide economic developments represent dimensions or sectors of creation's fullness. In attempting to assess the times in which we live, let us, therefore, honor the Lord both for the intrinsic goodness of creation as well as for his guidance of human history. However critical we may be of human irresponsibility and disobedience in these sectors of society, we must never become doomsayers about technology as such, or about government as such, or about markets as such. We may not demonize what God has given us. All these gifts have their own intrinsic calling and dignity before the Lord. John Calvin, who has been seriously misinterpreted and misunderstood,[2] was, for instance, quite convinced that markets should be seen as good gifts of the Creator because they are vehicles for human beings to serve one another in true solidarity. In equally exalted language, he praised civil government as the institution by which God offers a peaceful life to all. That is the purpose for which government may use the far-reaching power of the sword to uphold public justice.

There is a third important reason why we should not demonize the process of globalization. Christians must be careful to use *selective normative criteria* to make judgments about such complex developments. We have been speaking about economic, technological, political, and social changes, which manifest deep cultural and religious dimensions. Some economic changes might be positive while certain political changes are negative, and vice versa. We must not confound categories or make sweeping judgments of approval or disapproval when we should be making more precise and distinct judgments. At the same time, we may not isolate different aspects of life as if they have a complete life of their own apart from the rest of life under God's authority. The Reformation stressed the principle that no part of life may be understood as standing outside the directives—the commandments—of the living God, for he is not only Sovereign, he is also Lawgiver and Lifegiver. Economic life, for instance, is placed under the divine rule of *oikonomia*—good stewardship. Economic life is meant to deliver the fruits of human labor in a way that satisfies the needs of the people of this earth, and so it presupposes care or trusteeship of everything, including everyone entrusted to our responsibility.

It may surprise you to hear me speak not only of a trusteeship of everything but also of everyone. I do so intentionally, for the Greek word *oikonomia*, as used in the parables of Jesus, for example, always entails the well-being of those who work on the land. Good *oikonomia*, Jesus explained, implies that servants receive their food in time. We might think of failure to care for the needy as *unethical* behavior, but Scripture presents it primarily as *uneconomic* behavior, for the poor are entitled to share in the fruits of this creation, including rest and time to renew their energies, because the creation is the *oikos*—the household—of the Lord himself. Anyone who bears responsibility for others and violates the economic criterion of caring for those who labor will hear harsh words when the Lord of the land—the Lord of creation—returns.

The return of the Lord, who is the ultimate owner of the earth, is a theme that permeates the biblical texts that deal with human economy. Jesus interprets economic life as having an eschatological dimension from the outset. A judge stands at the end of all our economic efforts and institutions, for when the Lord comes back to his *oikos*—his creation—he will ask all persons and all nations to render an account of their economic behavior *(oikonomike)*. This same finality holds for the process of globalization. Perhaps we can frame it in terms of two contrasting action scenarios. In the first, human economic activity honors the worldwide diversity of God's good creation and prefigures the reign of the coming Lord[3]—the good Shepherd-King—who will do justice to the weak, protect the poor, and take care of the land. In the second scenario, human economic activity blurs all distinctions among the different spheres of life worldwide[4] and proceeds on the basis of the conviction that the fittest should survive, that victory should go to the strongest, and that might makes right. Approached in terms of these contrasting scenarios, the process of globalization can be seen properly as subject to divine scrutiny, measurable by criteria of God's *oikonomia*. That which might appear to be the most secular, most neutral sector of contemporary economic activity will be exposed for what it is. Its underlying presuppositions will come to light.

To test this proposed critical-normative approach, let's look more closely at international finance, one of the most closed and seemingly secular, neutral, and self-determined sectors of modern society, but also one of the most dynamic factors that is leading the process of globalization.

International Finance and Its Role in Globalization

In the world of international finance, we can see the co-incidence of at least two remarkable phenomena. The first is that the financial flows are concentrated in the Western hemisphere. In spite of the fact that so many pressing economic needs are evident in the South and the East, finance does not flow in those directions. The recently published *World Investment Report* of UNCTAD (1999) indicates that 91 percent of worldwide foreign direct investment flows to the United States, Europe, and Japan, while the poorest and most indebted nations receive scarcely any benefit. A second, even more remarkable phenomenon is the very unequal balance between the so-called "real sphere" and "financial sphere" in the international economy. It is a well-known fact that less than 5 percent of international money transfers occur for the purpose of buying and selling goods and services in the real sphere. The other 95 percent are pure financial transactions.

What is the significance of these two phenomena, and how are they related? Let me draw your attention to the inversion of the so-called pyramid of international finance. For generations, international finance had its basis in the real economy—in the processes of production, consumption, and trade of goods and services. That was the bottom of the pyramid. Finance represented the smaller top of the pyramid and consisted of credit transactions, trade in property claims, and the buying and selling of foreign fixed currencies. Today, however, the pyramid has been turned upside down. Due to the emergence of freely floating currencies and the invention of a whole series of financial derivatives such as options and futures (which are nothing more than expectations turned into money), an explosion has occurred in the sphere of financial flows. There is now a trillion-dollar circuit in international finance that is driven almost entirely by collective, subjective guesses about what will happen economically around the world. The guesses are heavily influenced by the judgments of top speculators and the warnings of bank presidents. The collective expectations of institutional and individual investors now steer not only the enormous volumes of circulating money but also to a high degree the course of real economies, for no real economy can grow without the presence of enough risk capital. We seem to have reached the point, then, where the financial economy is overtaking and determining the development of the real economy. The top and bottom of the pyramid have exchanged places. Financial expectations do more to influence the real economy than the other way around.

Some will say that all of this is simply a neutral development, merely a matter of new economic facts. But is that the case? George Soros, himself one of the leading financial speculators, has written a fascinating book about this new economic reality.[5] He explains, first of all, that the strange world of inbuilt circularity, in which international finance seems to steer itself, is indeed one of the main reasons why capital remains concentrated in the West. When Western financial speculators spot a slight upward change in the economies of the South, they can send billions of dollars in that direction, but just as quickly they will move their capital back to the West. In a recent interview, Soros spoke openly of an "uneven playing field" for the poorer countries, because they have to pay a large premium in higher interest rates in order to attract capital.[6] And if any penalty is to be paid, it will be paid by the developing countries.

Soros does more than describe this new factual reality, however. He looks to sources and causes. In his view, the real source of the problems associated with financial markets is the presence of an overly influential mechanistic worldview, especially in the science of economics. His diagnosis sounds like it could be Kuyper's: "Equilibrium theory in economics is based on a false analogy with physics. Market fundamentalists have [thus] a fundamentally flawed conception of how financial markets operate. They believe that financial markets tend toward equilibrium. [But] financial markets are inherently unstable. It is market fundamentalism that has put financial capital into the driver's seat."[7]

Soros makes an important point here, but something more needs to be said, for a mechanistic worldview does not stand on its own feet. It both manifests and fosters a mind-set of responsibility-avoidance. In teaching people to think and act in terms of a supposedly well-functioning machine—the market mechanism, the democratic mechanism, and the mechanisms of various social, political, and industrial plans—such teaching leaves out all questions of responsibility for the outcomes. The system—the machinery—supposedly produces outcomes automatically. Dietrich Bonhoeffer once made the remark that the question "Who?" is a question of transcendence; the question "How?" is one of immanence.[8]

This brings us to the first major point of our inquiry. To think of the world of finance as a "neutral sector" is obviously not self-evident or naturally inevitable. It is a deliberate construct, an intentional way of thinking. To think of financial flows as a neutral mechanism comes from a voluntarily constructed understanding of finance—and perhaps of economic life as a whole—as a closed universe. Nothing enters from outside the "mechanism."

Let me try to explain this in somewhat greater detail. If one starts with the idea that an economy and markets are autonomous, self-contained mechanisms, then it is quite logical that in the long run one will act in the world of finance as if functioning in a self-propelled, free-floating mechanism. In fact, we have seen precisely this course being taken in the development of the world's monetary systems. It started with the abandonment of the gold standard and continued through to the breakdown of the Bretton Woods agreements. Thus, there has been the gradual loosening of all restraints and directives from outside the "mechanism" of financial flows.

The logic of an autonomous world of finance would not be so significant or lead to such dramatic consequences if, indeed, the domain of money and credit stood on its own feet and had to bear responsibility only for itself. But that is not the case. I mentioned the enormous disadvantage of the poorest and most indebted countries, which lack necessary, low-priced capital. Especially in those countries, but also in others as well, there now exists a constant fear about what will happen in financial markets. Most governments have become painfully aware of their growing dependence on the whims of global capital, as if a new "big brother" is watching them. This is why countries have begun to compete so vigorously with one another by lowering their taxes, for example, just so they can attract foreign investments. No less a figure than Johan Witteveen, former managing director of the International Monetary Fund (IMF), warned explicitly against such a development. Moreover, he said that any further finance-led explosion of the world economy could result in irreparable destruction of the environment.[9]

Surely we would not anticipate harm to poorer countries and ecological destruction as consequences of living by the rules of good *oikonomia* that Jesus taught. These degradations also seem to conflict with the Reformation insight that no part or institution of human society should have control over all the others. Today, even basic welfare systems, environmental protections, and the availability of capital for poorer countries are jeopardized because these countries are far too dependent on the emerging global-finance superstructure, which in turn depends on nothing more than subjective expectations and speculations about the future. If financial expectations suddenly drop, then everything can go down. Thus, we live together now on the slopes of a financial volcano that sooner or later will erupt.

If this danger is real, why is there not a stronger political reaction to it? Many say that the reason is a lack of political will. But that is too superficial a reaction. I spoke earlier about the tendency among those committed to a mechanistic worldview to eschew or shrink from responsibility. Yet how far can such avoidance of responsibility go? Is it possible that we are no longer able to make a realistic appraisal of the consequences of our actions because we have formed the habit of trusting mechanisms to work? Are we, in other words, experiencing a partial paralysis as a result of the narrowing of the Western mind?

A century ago, Kuyper did not hesitate to speak of hypnosis when trying to describe the mind-set of his day. *Hypnosis,* according to the *Oxford English Dictionary,* is an artificially created sleep. From Kuyper's time until now, millions and millions of people have been strongly influenced if not hypnotized by the ideologies of communism, fascism, and capitalism. What do we really know about the development of the human spirit under these conditions? Faith in false gods may have distorted our minds and hearts more than we imagine.

To hypothesize that the Western mind has been narrowed and distorted could be very risky as well as far reaching. It needs to be tested. Let us return, then, to the complex global developments, but this time let's look especially at their structural and cultural components.

3

Structural and Cultural Dimensions of Globalization

A number of books have been published on globalization, and their titles refer to capitalism as the prevailing structure.[1] We must be careful, however, not to miss what is new about the present form of globalization. Take, for example, the matter of competition. Competition has always been recognized as one of the hallmarks of modern capitalism. Thus, it seems easy to conclude that globalization is simply another expression of capitalism, but now occurring at the global level. However, this conclusion overlooks two important features of the new international reality.

First of all, globalization manifests not only worldwide competition but also many kinds of increasing *cooperation.* Cooperation occurs not only in the business sector but also and even more remarkably in the growing number of civil movements. Millions of people are working together in new ways for the protection of human rights and the environment, for example (think of Amnesty International and Greenpeace). Others have organized out of concern for migrants and displaced persons or for the poor more generally (for example, Christian Aid and the Jubilee campaign to cancel the debts of the poorest countries). Several national labor unions have become more aware of their global responsibilities and are taking action to oppose unacceptable working conditions and the misuse of children. And governments themselves are finding new ways to cooperate on issues of environmental destruction (for example, the global conferences in Rio de Janeiro, 1992, and in Kyoto, 1998), which even in their limited achievements are helping to shape the international order.

Many of these movements are not rooted directly or even indirectly in Christian consciousness or intention. Nevertheless, they show degrees of responsiveness to God's commands of justice and stewardship, which are valid for all people. Therefore, we should be thankful for every cooperative act and movement on behalf of justice and stewardship that emerges, even when non-Christians take the lead and Christians stand aside.

Observing these cooperative movements, we must, therefore, refine our original hypothesis. It is not as broad and general as we supposed. At least some of the dynamics of contemporary world history show a tendency opposite to that of global capitalism. Nevertheless, in addition to growing worldwide cooperation there is also a second neglected dimension of global change that is the cause of far greater concern. It is the impact of growing competition on the structure of our entire societies, both in breadth and in depth.

The Breadth and Depth of Economic Competition

The *breadth* of the structural impact can be seen in the way that the formula of competition is now advocated in fields far outside the practice of business. There is increasing competition among schools, universities, sports organizations, orchestras, and even clinics and hospitals. Information and communication, once the heart of culture, have become important economic battlefields. Governments, as we mentioned, have also been forced to compete.[2] In the European Union, the term "policy competition" is the standard expression for the contest among national governments to reach the highest level of competitiveness in the union.

Reformed Christians typically notice the violation of the principle of sphere sovereignty when government oversteps its bounds. Indeed, the state can easily become a totalitarian threat to the callings of other institutions and to economic freedom. But this should not blind us to the fact that the opposite is also possible. The sphere of economic life, driven by the hard rules of competitiveness, can also develop totalitarian features and violate the family's and the state's spheres of responsibility.

This is the juncture at which we need to recognize the *depth* of the structural impact of economic competition. The classical economic understanding of competition is that of producers competing to satisfy the *existing* demands of consumers. But this is fast becoming an outdated concept. Due to the revolution in information technology, competition has now shifted to the field of influencing and changing consumer demand itself. For example, a titanic struggle, to use Dan Schiller's words,[3] is now taking place between giant multinational communications companies to gain control over the Internet with its seven hundred million telephone connections. These companies expect the Internet to become the entrance key to the homes of all modern consumers, and the conglomerate that holds that key will wield unbelievable economic power. This new economy of immaterial services does not aim first for the body but for the head and the mind.[4] Or as Joseph S. Nye and Admiral William A. Owens put it in a *Foreign Affairs* article, information is the "new money" of the global economy, and the countries that prove best at controlling the information revolution will be the most powerful.[5]

For the new global economy to continue its rapid progress, in other words, it needs to create as its environment a new public consciousness. It needs its own domain where it can cultivate and steer consumer demands by means of endless flows of well-organized information. The fact that such a "system-need" now exists is one of the most remarkable recent changes in the style of competition. There has now arisen a need to create new scarcities in an artificial way by influencing the human mind itself.

It is true, of course, that human needs expand with new kinds of economic development. New possibilities create new opportunities. This is the cultural dimension of economic growth. However, in a multidimensional society, corporate-demand managers should not have overarching control of an entire culture, any more than the church or the state should have supreme control. Demand-management is nonetheless becoming one of the deep structural characteristics of the entire Western economy.

The Risks Associated with Economic Competition

The new competitiveness just described could not have emerged without a strong rationale, without a driving motivation, behind it. That rationale or drive is the same as in the world of finance, namely, the desire for autonomy and the affirmation of the self.[6] Imagine what would happen if consumers began to show signs of satiation and satisfaction with what they have. Would it not threaten the foundations of growth for the whole economy and, in turn, threaten our economic and political power?

If the loss or decline of economic and political power seems risky to those of us in the West, the risks involved in continuing on our present course are far greater—for the poor nations, for the world's entire ecosystem, and for our own spiritual and mental health. The poor are in danger because the aim to create artificial scarcity will sooner or later prevent the alleviation of real scarcity. The resources and capital needed to feed and house the needy will no longer be available. The earth is not big enough to satisfy all the desires that can be produced and stimulated by the information circuits of a postmodern society. The 1999 *World Development Report* from the World Bank says that in the year 2000, 1.5 billion people will live below the poverty level of $1.00 income per day. (In 1987, it was 1.2 billion.)

The environment is also endangered, which threatens everyone. Our energy-intensive patterns of production and consumption appear to be causing serious climate change, leading to more soil erosion, more floods, and even more locusts.[7] The space now needed for the disposal of garbage from a city the size of London is 140 times its own size, almost the space of the whole of Great Britain.

Finally, the present course threatens all of us, the rich included. A kind of virtual reality is now under construction in which a religiously deep myth of autonomous, limitless self-aggrandizement drives us into an ever narrower tunnel. Our minds become closed to alternatives because we believe that the present course is an economic necessity.[8] The tune of economic progress is repeated over and over like a new Psalm 23: "I shall not want, for growth is with us . . ." The soft voices of commercials assure us that it is good to have more and more, for only in that way can the economy and finance keep on expanding. A collective hypnosis sets in.

This moment, at the turn of the millennium, appears to me to be one of the most critical points in human history. Powerful, untruthful, hypnotic ideologies corrupted societies and destroyed millions of people throughout the twentieth century. Yet none of them had the instruments of communication available to it to infiltrate the human mind the way the present ideology of limitless economic and technological expansion can do.[9] Human subjectivity seems to be enthroned with god-like power, yet the human spirit is, at the same time, increasingly objectified (turned into a manipulated economic object) and brought under the control of a seemingly inescapable necessity. It reminds me of Friedrich Nietzsche's famous parable about the madman who enters the marketplace carrying a lantern and proclaiming the death of God.[10] From now on, he says to his astonished listeners, you have entered a higher history, for who gave you the power to wipe out the horizon and to exchange it for one of your own design? Who gave you the power to disconnect the earth from the sun and to live by the light of your own lantern? Those with the power to do this have indeed become gods. The madman then looked his audience in the eye and asked them an extremely frightening question: But doesn't this also mean that from now on we can fall without any restraint and that darkness will encompass us and it will become colder and colder? For if we ourselves have to play God and act like God, what then will happen with this earth and with ourselves?

4

Breaking Free from the Hypnosis of Our Age

The path we have been following has led us to the deepest level of society and its culture: the religious foundation or root. We could sense it when we were following the drift of finance toward ever greater autonomy. Now we can see how that claim arises from the tendency to make competition and competitiveness the universal law for all of society. Yet, in order to enforce this law, humans must be willing to subject themselves to new styles of life based on the religiously deep conviction that more is always better than less and that "there is no alternative" (TINA).[1] If this is true about what dominates the global economy, then clearly there is nothing religiously neutral about economics.[2] For if it is true that we now live at the borderline of the imprisonment of the human spirit itself, then in principle every human institution can and will be sucked into the competitive whirlpool. Therefore, it is also true that our civilization has arrived at a new crossroads of conflicting religious drives.

We must be careful, however, as we take up the question of the religious direction being taken by our societies. In order for a society to move in the right direction—in the way of truth and life—the meaning of each dimension of life must be disclosed, not closed off. Such disclosure is possible only by following the way of obedience to God-given norms in all areas of life, including economics. Moving in the direction of self-chosen autonomy restricts and closes off life's meaning by leading to the violation of the norms of stewardship, justice, and love. Thus, for a society to choose the correct religious direction it is not a question of its members simply joining movements that fight big-business interests. Nor can the question of religious direction be reduced to choosing the right political camp. The whole of society, not just part of it, needs to be opened up.

These are weighty words, I realize, and they may seem to foster hopelessness. Are we now locked into a nightmare? No, the diagnosis we are offering actually helps point the way out of the predicament. For it to do that, however, we must wake up. We may not hide from the final consequences of our deeds but must have faces once again. With this I mean not only that it is not fitting for the children of light to be found asleep. I mean something more, namely, that we need an awakening of Christianity as in the great revival movements of the past. Awakening in this sense implies the willingness to stand up to be addressed by God and our fellow human beings, as C. S. Lewis explains in his book *Till We Have Faces*.[3] We must wake up and leave childhood behind and accept mature responsibility, in the way that Bonhoeffer explained the meaning of the word *Mundigkeit*.[4] Or to say it in the language of the Book of Job, we need to gird ourselves so we can learn to listen. One of the oldest Christian hymns says, "Wake up, O sleeper, rise from the dead, and Christ will shine on you" (Eph. 5:14). Could it be that Christ himself forms with his body the crossroads of our time?

A Plan for Reformation and Transformation

Consider carefully the case I am making. Standing in contrast to the mechanistic, childish, passively accommodating, and fearful view of our time is the possibility of a view that is fully awake, mature, realistic, and open-faced, in terms of which we may accept new responsibilities with joy and confidence. It is this second outlook and approach that we need, because it opens our eyes to the coming of a different Master and thus implies a turn toward the inner reformation, and not just an outer revision, of our present societies and economies.

From the point of view of such a new awakening, I see five aspects of reformation and transformation, five steps we have to take that could bring us back to a good style of globalization, corresponding to the above-mentioned scenario that leads to the survival of the weak.

1. First of all, mature and awakened people cannot and will not be blind to the extreme forms of childishness that have crept into our consumption-oriented culture. Children always seem to want more even if they do not need it, and they strive to keep what they have. Maturation means leaving such childishness behind by learning to live with restraints and affirming others. Childishness of unlimited desires, however, colors most consumption styles, including those of Christians in the rich countries. This exists hand in hand with the contrary experience of millions of people in poorer countries who lack necessities and are left unaffirmed by the rich countries. Neither the rich nor the poor, however, will find happiness as a fruit of an endless consumption rivalry. Real abundance means literally that one has more than one's cup can hold. It means having more than enough. A culture in which people have lost the sense of "enough" is also a culture that loses its awareness of abundance. The outcome is a never fully satisfying "enjoyment" of luxury (the Greek word *luxury* means "distortion"), a distortion that can grow in and shape the human heart.

The first step we need to take, therefore, is to awaken from our sleep, our hypnosis, and realize that sufficiency—being satisfied with enough—is not a curse but a blessing. Among other things, learning to be satisfied with enough

buys back time, time that is now used in the consumption
of so many goods, so we can enjoy more fully what we do
have and the richness of human experience. More time also
allows us to participate in counter-hypnotic movements so
that the self-manufactured goal of unlimited material expansion can gradually be replaced by the goal of enough, of
sufficiency. This is what the Sabbath laws of Israel were all
about. Rest and shalom were a gift from God, the precondi-
tion for work rather than the result or achievement of endless work. We, too, need to accept rest and sufficiency as
gifts and not expect more from our productivity and consumption than Israel was to expect from theirs.

2. The second step we need to take is closely related to
the first. It is not enough simply to give up the aspiration
toward limitless consumption. Lowering consumption by itself might even destabilize our economies. A wise and mature attitude toward consumption will also have its consequences at the level of the wages and profits people desire.
Workers, managers, and shareholders who fight only for the
highest possible financial rewards are immature, for the
most meaningful purposes in life can be achieved only
through restraint, through the diminution rather than the
expansion of claims.

The Hebrew language has a beautiful word, *bechinnom*,
which means offering something for nothing, giving with
open hands. The great Jewish thinker Friedrich Weinreb
once said of *bechinnom* that nothing else can save the
world.[5] Christians can see the truth of this statement in the
life and death of Jesus. And it has an important bearing on
economic life. If there is nothing in economic life besides
the exchange of something for something else, then the
adult power to withhold claims and restrain oneself can
never come to the fore. Yet the preservation of the poor and
the weak always depends to some degree on acts of restraint
on the part of the rich.[6]

The Dutch polder model of development, which is well
known in the world because of its positive results for em-

ployment and environmental protection, is a partial illustration of the power to withhold and the wisdom of giving with open hands. The model is built on two foundations, both of which stem from the Christian social movement in Europe. The first is the long-standing cooperation between employers and employees undertaking joint efforts for the common good. The second is voluntary wage restraint on the part of labor unions in order to serve broader, labor-related purposes. These foundations are alien to a mechanistic, individualistic approach to the economy but fit completely with a mature, organic economy.

3. The third step to take toward maturity is to move our Western economies from purely expansive types to full-blossoming types. *Expansion* is a word that suggests simply trying to do the same thing faster and faster. It is more of a mechanistic concept. *Blossoming*, by contrast, is an organic metaphor, which suggests, for example, the organic cooperation of cells in a fruit tree. A tree does not use all of its energy simply to keep growing taller. It channels some of it into producing blossoms and fruit. Abraham Kuyper liked to contrast mechanistic and organic metaphors.

For economic life, this contrast suggests the following: Growth, for mature people, means learning to do new things, not simply doing old things faster with the aim of getting more of the same. At times, less consumption growth and a reduction in income demands can be a way to store up reserves that will be needed for new forms of economic development oriented to a far stronger preventive care for people and nature both inside and outside the production process. Some of the decisions I am talking about have to be made by business and labor. In other cases, government must act to make sure that the environment is preserved and that other aims besides maximum financial return control the economy. The fight against world hunger, for meaningful employment, for better health care and educational opportunity—all of these can blossom when entrepreneurial energy is not focused solely on maximizing financial return.

4. There is a fourth step to take. Some might say that my comments about a blossoming economy are idealistic and impractical. Perhaps on a local level where people know each other they will restrain themselves in favor of another person. Perhaps this can happen in a church community, as John Perkins has demonstrated in Mississippi and elsewhere with microenterprise development to empower the poor. But surely this can't happen on a global scale, can it? The answer is that we need to overcome the prejudice that national and global markets are inevitably impersonal and anonymous and that market rules govern us as an external fate, for the anonymity of the market is often not natural but only man-made. Corporations, after all, are more than cold-hearted Molochs; they should be seen and valued as human institutions. If anywhere, then here, indeed, an awakened and more adult view is needed, a view that goes beyond ideological divisions and categories. Mature adults are willing to present their faces to one another, to be recognized by one another as responsible human beings, willing to look behind supposedly anonymous structures and facades to find out how to address other human beings in true co-responsibility.

Let me say it another way. C. S. Lewis once described hell as the place where people keep moving farther and farther away from one another because each person is closed in by his or her own perceptions. Economic life becomes a hell if people remain locked in by the conviction that they must simply submit to market forces that are assumed to be inevitable and anonymous. If people cannot get beyond their prejudice that life is determined by class struggle, or that business people are born evildoers, or that markets are governed mechanistically, then there can be no inner reformation of the economy because there can be no inner reformation of ourselves.

However, if and when we break through as awakened adults to call these prejudices into question, wonderful things can happen. For example, some environmental organizations have begun to overcome the barrier of assuming that they must always fight businesses as enemies. Instead, they are working to understand the value of mutual contracts with large corporations. In some cases, they are even forming copartnerships with companies that want to change course toward greater environmental protection.[7]

Another example is the Brent Spar incident. When the Shell oil corporation intended to dump an obsolete oil platform into the Atlantic Ocean, a public outcry arose. Even ministers of the German cabinet joined the action to boycott Shell gasoline stations. The reaction caught Shell off guard, as a total surprise, leading it to question how it could so easily have misinterpreted public opinion. In 1997, Dutch Shell decided to invite the Dutch Council of Churches to join in an open dialogue about these matters. The council accepted the invitation in the spirit of the ecumenical theme of "mission in foreign structures," which had been adopted at the World Council of Churches Assembly in Canberra, Australia. In three sessions together, each organization discovered the face of the other. Shell even revised its corporate code.[8]

Another kind of positive development has been fostered by a Christian entrepreneur in Great Britain, George Goyder. Goyder proposed years ago to give special recognition to companies that demonstrate a high degree of responsibility for their workers, consumers, suppliers from less developed countries, and the environment by giving them the official title "public company."[9] I believe this idea should be revived and taken a step further—to grant the title of "publicly authorized company" (PAC) to those companies that receive a positive recommendation from at least one environmental organization, one labor union, one consumer organization, and one civic movement. The charm of this proposal is that it would encourage corporations to develop traits that also begin to define for the public the traits of a good economy. Consumers can also then begin to make choices in favor of these traits by purchasing products from PACs. This in turn would encourage other companies to change in positive ways. Thus, producers, consumers, unions, and civic movements would all be challenged to present their faces to one another.

5. The final step we need to take concerns the responsibility of governments and international law. It is certainly the case that the present crisis in world finance and the impact of global information technology depend on political decisions. What can we expect from our governments, given the fact that they, too, have been influenced and even shaped by the tendency to structure public life in accord with the rules of an economic mechanism?

I see constructive possibilities if they, too, wake up. Governments stand directly under the high command of the Lord of heaven and earth. They have been called to act in the Lord's name to uphold justice and, when necessary, to use the power of the sword to overcome oppression of the weak and injustice in the broader society. It is childish and even cowardly for governments to hide from this mandate and to run away from their responsibility out of fear of what other powers might think or do. Governments must wake up and act in a mature way to develop statecraft—the art of shaping just public communities, including a global community. Three avenues are open before us.

- The first avenue that governments must take is to reform *international finance.* It is a mistake to think of finance as an independent sphere of life in which government should not interfere. Money is a publicly produced and regulated instrument of economic transaction. It functions properly only if it serves the public good. If humans turn money into an idol—Mammon—it becomes a very cruel master. In order to promote international justice, the world's governments ought to meet as soon as possible, as they did at Bretton Woods following World War II, to chain or tame the wild animal of global finance before it breaks out of its cage entirely.

The present "order" of global finance has become a standard example of disorder. It is breaking up all stable economic relationships in the community of nations. Public finance must be grounded once again in real economic life to meet the needs of the real economy for international liquidity. My deep hope is that in this conference, the rich nations will have the wisdom and maturity to diminish their own claims on international money in order to give poorer countries more access to it and enable them to pay off their remaining debts, so that just as in Israel's year of Jubilee they can make a new, debt-free start. Such action would bring a blessing to the entire world. What a recovery it would be if it could begin with the healing of the poorest nations.

- Second, governments need to act to structure the *global network of information and technology* so that it serves the public good and not only the interests of some private parties. The information-technology network is similar to money in some respects. It should serve the public as a whole. If it becomes the private playing field of monopolistic powers, it can become a cruel master that intrudes on the privacy of others in a deeply destructive way. The United States, for example, which has the leading information technology sectors, should not postpone too long helping to establish the international protective and distributive measures that will prevent the subjugation of human consciousness to the expanding control of private commercial interests. If ever there was a need for a confrontation for the sake of public well-being, it is here.

- A third avenue down which governments need to move in order to do justice is to *protect the world's ecosystem*. Why is the global ecosystem in such danger? Is it because the earth has become too small to meet the needs of its growing population? No, it is because humans are too small; they are failing to act with full responsibility. Ghandi once said that there is enough for everyone's need but not enough for everyone's greed. If this is accepted as the guideline, then the environmental crisis can also be solved. Let me make this as clear as possible. The formulation of national and international environmental policies should *not* start with the promise and the faith that technology will save us. It should start at the point of greatest weakness, namely, to protect—to put fences around—those natural endowments that are needed to sustain the life of future generations and animal species. To preserve life for the future means being willing to guard the carrying capacity of the globe as public commons.

Our Ultimate Hope

When Jesus rose from the dead, he took a fish and ate it in front of his disciples. Thus, two millennia ago, new life, invincible life, took part in our sinful human economy. Since his resurrected life entered our world's economic patterns, consumption is no longer the same and production can no longer be the same. Everything has now become relative in the deepest sense of that word, for Jesus is now the Life, and no part of life may ever again become an absolute.

What I have written here is built on the deep conviction that in following the way of life opened by the risen Jesus, we may find the way out of our self-imposed, childish, and destructive patterns of economic life. If our societies seek to maintain the present way of life absolutely, without change, they will certainly perish. They will not be able to endure in the context of their own self-created hypnotic universe. But those societies that learn to lose their lives by acts of restraint and sharing will find that they not only survive but also flourish. For a new King is already on his way to let us share in his abundance.

The Entire World Needs to Be Awakened

Response by Brian Fikkert

"Wake up from your hypnosis, Western civilization!" cries Bob Goudzwaard in his Kuyper Lecture to close out the millennium. The first time I heard Goudzwaard's call to wake up was in 1983, when I was enrolled at Dordt College, the site of this year's Kuyper Lecture. I was taking my first course in economics and was quite enamored with the standard textbook material, which described the wonders of Western capitalism using elegant mathematics and diagrams. I was finding the mathematical rigor and precision of this social science quite appealing. Its conclusion—that laissez-faire capitalism is the "best" economic system—sat well with my own preconceived notions. Although I should have known better, I was also

Brian Fikkert is associate professor of economics at Covenant College, Lookout Mountain, Georgia, where he established the Chalmers Center to promote microenterprise development in poorer countries. He earned his Ph.D. at Yale University and taught at the University of Maryland before going to Covenant.

drawn to the discipline's claims that its conclusions are morally neutral. My introductory textbook claimed that it was simply describing the way things really are and that it was not making any value judgments about the way things ought to be. The "fact" of the matter is simply that laissez-faire capitalism is "best," and the textbook had all the mathematical formulae to prove it. It had not occurred to me that my textbook's assertion that laissez-faire capitalism is "best" presupposed some sort of ethical standard for ranking alternative economic systems. In short, I had been hypnotized.

I can still remember sitting in the library reading the assigned portion of Goudzwaard for the first time and being quite irritated with him. I liked my hypnotic sleep and did not want to be awakened. Yet, I could not deny Goudzwaard's assertions that economic life—like everything else in creation—is not morally neutral but is normed. The Creator of the universe saw everything that he had made, and he alone could pronounce it "good." He set the standards, not we ourselves. Furthermore, when one considers the norms that the Creator has revealed in his Word, it is clear that laissez-faire capitalism—like every economic system in a fallen world—has both strengths and weaknesses. Being awakened from my hypnosis was painful and did not happen overnight. Indeed, the process is ongoing, as I am prone to sleepiness!

Given that Goudzwaard's work continues to challenge me to wake up, I am humbled at being asked to respond to his latest sounding of the alarm bells. I urge readers to consider carefully all that he has said and to work communally to awaken not just the West but the entire world from its slumber. In that spirit, I would like to present several points that I hope will make some small contribution to this effort.

Globalization and Its Religious Roots

In his consideration of globalization, Goudzwaard surveys the factual processes of the global economy, tries to determine the structural and cultural framework that produces these phenomena, and then probes for the foundational religious drives underlying these structures. In the first stage, Goudzwaard highlights the fact that capital mobility and changes in information technology have created a world that is increasingly interconnected, the result being that events that take place in one region necessarily impact people on the other side of the globe. Of particular concern is that small changes in investors' perceptions of the likely financial returns of investing in various countries can result in massive capital movements in a matter of minutes. For example, a slight rise in U.S. interest rates could trigger an exodus of funds from Asia to the United States, destabilizing governments as well as the business community in Asia and influencing the lives of millions of workers, particularly the poor in the Two-Thirds World. One of the most disturbing things to Goudzwaard is that westerners are not unsettled by this. Rather, they have been hypnotized by the notion that these processes are natural, and therefore, both morally neutral and unavoidable.

In the second stage of Goudzwaard's analysis, in which he probes for the structural and cultural framework that supports globalization, he notes that modern capitalism legitimizes competition, encouraging investors to move massive amounts of capital as they seek to defeat their competitors. The hypnotized Western mind views such behavior as natural and morally neutral, never holding these investors or the system in which they operate accountable for the fact that competition in financial markets may be ruining millions of lives.

Finally, Goudzwaard probes for the religious foundations of these processes and social structures, arguing that they are based on the conviction that "more is always better than less" and that "there is no alternative" because the very nature of being human is to want more in order to fulfill oneself.

Tempering this rather bleak picture, Goudzwaard cites examples of cooperative behavior in which various parties have apparently sought the public good above and beyond their narrow self-interests.

Goudzwaard concludes by offering an alternative path that will lead to a more just process of globalization in which the weak can survive. This path is characterized by people being satisfied with what they have rather than always wanting more, showing restraint in their demands for higher wages or profits, moving away from a fascination with economic expansion, recognizing that economic processes involve people with faces and not just impersonal market forces, and establishing international treaties governing finance, technology, and the environment.

Awakening to the "Now but Not Yet"

One of the greatest challenges for Christians who are seeking to formulate just public policies is to remain awake to the "now but not yet" of the kingdom of God. Although Christ reigns as King over the universe right now, the full manifestation of that kingdom will not be seen until he comes again. It is at that point alone that every knee will bow and every tongue will confess that Christ does indeed own every square inch of the universe. Living between the times presents special challenges for Christians. On the one hand, if we focus only on the "not yet" of the kingdom, we are prone to retreat from engagement in cultural activity, throwing up our hands in despair that nothing can be done until Christ returns. On the other hand, if we forget that the full manifestation of the kingdom is not yet at hand, we may become overly optimistic about what can actually be accomplished prior to the kingdom's consummation.

Part of living with this tension is, prophetically, to point a fallen world to the claims of the King of Kings while simultaneously recognizing—in our programs and in our policies—that the universe and its inhabitants are infected and distorted by sin. To ignore this reality is costly, as it results in the design of policies that cannot work and that may actually do harm to the very people they were intended to help. A case in point is many of the welfare policies implemented in the United States over the past three decades, which—although well intentioned—failed to take into account the sinfulness of the human heart in both the poor and those who administered the programs.

I would have appreciated a clearer articulation from Goudzwaard of how this tension informs his suggested steps for bringing "reformation and transformation" to the globalization process. Consider again Goudzwaard's program. Goudzwaard is calling for the West to wake up from its hypnosis and to take responsibility for stewarding the Lord's resources in a way that brings economic justice. Goudzwaard argues that this will necessarily involve a major reorientation of the West's fundamental, religious commitment to autonomy and self-gratification. If this reorientation happens, Goudzwaard sees constructive possibilities for governments to establish international treaties regulating international finance, technology, and the environment.

In view of the "now but not yet" nature of the kingdom, I have several concerns about the way Goudzwaard has articulated his program for reformation of the globalization process. My suspicion is that Goudzwaard would not disagree fundamentally with my concerns, so perhaps these should best be considered qualifications to what he has said.

First, at times Goudzwaard appears to argue that adopting international treaties governing finance, technology, and the environment is contingent upon a major inner transformation of our societies and governments so that they forsake their fundamental, religious commitments to autonomy and self-gratification. In my view, the inner transformation that Goudzwaard is appropriately longing for is so profound that it can be accomplished only if there is widespread conversion to Christ and his lordship. Short of this happening, where does Goudzwaard's program leave us? Are there not steps that could be taken even if there is not widespread conversion to Christ? Is it really the case that progress on international treaties is contingent upon this inner transformation actually occurring? Is it not possible that God's common grace might enable unbelievers to see the wisdom of "waking up" without a profound transformation of their fundamental religious commitments? Furthermore, are there other driving forces—even the pursuit of self-interest—that could propel nations to agree to regulate the international economy? At times, Goudzwaard seems to answer both of the latter two questions in the affirmative, since he sees the global environmental conferences at Rio de Janeiro and Kyoto as not being "rooted directly or even indirectly in Christian consciousness or intention." At other times, however, he appears to argue that this inner transformation must precede progress on international treaties.

My second concern is closely related to the first. If one believes that profound inner transformation must precede international cooperation, then one must necessarily interpret instances of cooperation as indicators that an inner transformation has actually taken place. Goudzwaard comes close to suggesting this when he says that the Rio de Janeiro and Kyoto conferences "show degrees of responsiveness to God's commands of justice and stewardship." Perhaps. But it is also possible that such international cooperation is proceeding from motives other than a responsiveness to God's commands.

Why does this matter? As I mentioned earlier, how we design policies reflects our assumptions concerning the motivations of individuals, organizations, and nations. If we naively assume that an apparent desire for cooperation at an international level reflects some turning away from selfishness on the part of individuals and nations, we may fail to build in the appropriate safeguards to curb future actions emanating from impure motives.

Consider for example one of the most successful pieces of international "cooperation" ever produced, the General

Agreement on Tariffs and Trade (GATT), which has now evolved into the World Trade Organization (WTO). Established at the end of World War II, signatory countries to GATT bound themselves to rules designed to expand the benefits of international trade across the globe. On the surface, one could say that this is an example of international cooperation in which nations put aside their selfishness and even gave up some of their national sovereignty to promote justice and stewardship.

In my view, this would be a naive interpretation. Countries agreed to GATT's rules because they believed that doing so was in their own self-interest, not because they were responding to God's commands for stewardship and justice. Indeed, the moment when Western nations in general and the United States in particular felt that the rules of the game were no longer in their own interest, they repeatedly and flagrantly violated these rules or pressured the Two-Thirds World into agreeing to changes in the rules. In fact, the only reason GATT has been successful at all is because its architects correctly assumed that both nations and the politicians who run them were prone to pursue their own perceived self-interest. As a result, the architects of GATT designed the entire process for multilateral trade negotiations around the notion that little would be accomplished unless all parties believed they were gaining from this process. If they had not correctly perceived that pursuit of self-interest dominates the motivations of people and nations, they would have designed GATT's structure very differently, the result being that it would have been far less effective than it has been.

In light of these considerations, when Goudzwaard calls for an international conference to enable the Two-Thirds World to make a new debt-free start, we must proceed with caution. Although I am in favor of debt relief for these countries, particularly since many of their debt problems are the direct result of actions taken by the U.S. Federal Reserve Board, the design of a debt relief program must take into account the fallen nature of both the lenders and the borrowers if it is to truly help the poorest countries of the world. For example, what incentive will commercial banks in the West have to lend to the Two-Thirds World in the future if they know that there is a precedent for such loans to be "forgiven" by Western governments? A policy intended to help the Two-Thirds World could actually hurt in the long run if it causes self-interested bankers to withhold future credit. Similarly, what is the message to borrowers in the Two-Thirds World, many of which are corrupt governments, if they are not held responsible for those instances in which they have poorly handled the money they have borrowed? Does debt forgiveness in this case encourage future misbehavior on the part of ruling elites, causing further harm to the poor living under their rule? I am far more comfortable with treaties that assume sinful motivations on the part of individuals and governments than treaties designed under the assumption that the relevant actors are cooperating as a result of "responsiveness to God's commands of justice and stewardship." We live in the "not yet," and our design of treaties must reflect this. This, too, is part of being fully awake.

Waking Up the West Is Not Enough

One might get the impression from reading Goudzwaard that the central problem facing the Two-Thirds World is the West's blind faith in a mechanistic process that implicitly legitimizes self-aggrandizement and autonomy. Although I am in agreement with Goudzwaard that the issues he has raised are extremely important, there are other factors that appear to me to be equally, if not more important, for the progress of the Two-Thirds World. Let me be clear: There is no question that many historic and contemporary actions of both the governments and the private sectors in the Western world have done tremendous harm to the poor in the Two-Thirds World. There is real structural evil in the international arena, and an unrestrained globalization process poses serious threats to the stability and health of many nations. However, it does not follow that the West is the only or even the primary problem to be overcome if the poorest of the poor are to be helped. In fact, there is plenty of blame to go around, and more than just the West needs to be awakened from its commitment to the status quo.

Let us consider one of the most vulnerable members of the world's community, a girl born to a Hindu family in rural India. From the moment of her birth, Romita is a disappointment to her family, which has strong cultural and religious biases in favor of boys. In fact, 73 million such baby girls are currently "missing" in India. When food is scarce, Romita is likely to be given less food than her brothers, a situation that will affect her cognitive, physical, social, and emotional status for the remainder of her life. If any of the children in the family are able to go to school, the parents will choose Romita's brothers first.

Romita's parents, who have little education and struggle with their own health on a daily basis, try to make a living through the cultivation of a small plot of land using primitive techniques. Better techniques are available, but the Hindu worldview promotes accepting one's lot in life, so Romita's parents are not predisposed to search for change. Even if they did want to improve their situation, as members of a lower caste, they are locked into their current socioeconomic status by both the formal and informal institutions in their region.

Romita's parents once tried to get a $30 loan to purchase a better plow, but the small size of their loan and their lack of acceptable collateral precluded them from obtaining a loan from the formal banking sector. The money lender in their village—a loan shark—was willing to provide them with the capital, but he charged 400 percent interest per year.

Recently, there was a lot of excitement in the village because the extension agent from a multinational seed company had come through, demonstrating how his company's new seed could double crop yields. Unfortunately, the seeds will no longer be available because India's nationalist government is forcing all foreign firms out of the country and is banning imports from abroad as well. The villagers' only option is to buy inferior seeds at a higher price from the government-owned seed monopoly.

Why is Romita poor? What is the solution? Is Goudzwaard correct that reducing the volatility of international capital flows will help the overall macroeconomic environment in which she lives? Yes. Has colonialism, both past and present, injured her? Certainly. There is plenty of sin in international economic structures. But Romita is also a victim of the sins of her parents, her community, and her nation, and it is likely that her own sins in the future will contribute to her poverty. Is Goudzwaard correct that the West needs to be less greedy? Of course, but it is not clear how a reduction in such greed will translate into a better life for Romita. If I eat one less hamburger today, will Romita somehow be better off? How? What is the mechanism by which my willingness to share can translate into gains for Romita, given that the obstacles to her advancement are so multifaceted in nature? Clearly, Western greed is only part of the problem. A comprehensive, holistic approach that involves many different institutions and addresses not just the material but also the spiritual, social, and psychological dimensions of poverty is desperately needed.

The encouraging news is that the international development community is starting to recognize this. For fifty years the approach of the World Bank to the Two-Thirds World has been based on the assumption that promoting free markets and pumping in more capital will stimulate economic growth, which will eventually trickle down to meet the needs of the poorest of the poor. Although the World Bank has made many contributions to the development process, its narrow approach, which tends to reduce reality to purely material and economic forces, has often proved ineffective in either generating growth or in ensuring that such growth actually helps the poorest of the poor. Its one-size-fits-all approach has been blind to the importance of local culture and institutions in determining both the overall impacts and the distributional consequences of its programs. Of course, the fact that these cultures and institutions are derived from and reinforced by worldviews that may or may not be conducive to development has been completely beyond the scope of the World Bank's thinking.

However, in 1999's *World Development Report,* the annual publication in which the World Bank gives its assessment of the state of the development process, the Bank made the following startling summary:

> Fifty years of development experience have yielded four critical lessons. First, macroeconomic stability is an essential prerequisite for achieving the growth needed for development. Second, growth does not trickle down; development must address human needs directly. Third, no one policy will trigger development; a comprehensive approach is needed. Fourth, institutions matter; sustained development should be rooted in processes that are socially inclusive and responsive to changing circumstances.[1]

Furthermore, at a conference in Kenya in March 2000, Roger Sullivan, the World Bank Sector Manager for Poverty Reduction and Social Development, said the World Bank is reviewing its policies and is considering how to partner with churches. Sullivan stated that the World Bank recognizes that the church can be a powerful ally in addressing poverty, due not only to its proximity to the poor in the grassroots communities but also to the fact that the church addresses all facets of human needs, including the spiritual.

Coming from the World Bank, these are remarkable assertions, and this type of thinking opens up opportunities for the Christian community to play a unique role in the development process, particularly by working at the grassroots level to complement the macroeconomic changes being fostered by the World Bank. More about the respective roles of various agents will be discussed further below.

Christians Need to Be Awakened Too

Goudzwaard asserts that the foundation for global capitalism rests on the West's commitment to the notion that more is better and that there is no alternative. Although this analysis is an accurate description of the West as a whole, it does not accurately describe the rather staunch commitment of many evangelicals to laissez-faire capitalism, a commitment that many would argue is based on scriptural principles. In fact, many Christians would be shocked to learn of Goudzwaard's criticisms of capitalism and outraged at his call for a harnessing of the market through international treaties. Hence, if the evangelical community is to join with Goudzwaard in calling for the West to wake up, these basic theological differences will need to be overcome first.

Space does not permit a complete discussion of contemporary evangelical thought regarding laissez-faire capitalism and socialism,[2] but the followers of Abraham Kuyper do not find themselves comfortable with either of these extremes for several reasons. First, as mentioned earlier, the "not yet" aspect of the kingdom implies that we live in a fallen world in which no system will be perfect. This basic biblical insight is in sharp contrast to the utopian visions of many proponents of capitalism and socialism, systems that are necessarily fraught with problems in a fallen world. Recognizing that no system is perfect reduces dogmatism and allows for the consideration of alternative policies and approaches that may be more or less appropriate in different cultural and institutional settings.

Second, Kuyper's commitment to sphere sovereignty—the notion that God has created a range of institutions, each of which has its own God-given nature and task—gives the

Kuyperian a reason to question both the socialist and the laissez-faire agendas. The former is suspect because it leads the state to usurp the legitimate roles of the individual, family, business, and so on, while the latter is suspect because it elevates individual autonomy over God-ordained spheres for the community and state. Hence, instead of demonizing either the state or the private sector, the followers of Kuyper believe that upholding the integrity of both are integral parts of being faithful stewards of God's good creation.

Turning our attention to capitalism for a moment, evangelical advocates of laissez-faire capitalism would do well to consider the basic philosophical presuppositions of capitalism's main proponents. As mentioned earlier, mainstream economic analysis—the neoclassical school of thought—claims that it is a value-free, morally neutral science that simply describes, in mathematical terms, the way things really are.[3] In actuality, neoclassical economics implicitly applies an ethical standard called "pareto efficiency," which says that an economic exchange between two parties is "good" if it is mutually beneficial, i.e., if it makes one person better off and the other person no worse off than he or she was before the exchange. The key point here is that the people themselves determine the extent to which they are better or worse off in each situation.

For example, assume that a firm is willing to hire Joe for $6/hour and that Joe is willing to work as long as he gets $4/hour. If the firm and Joe agree on a labor contract in which Joe works for $5/hour, then both the firm ($6-$5=$1) and Joe ($5-$4=$1) gain $1/hour from the exchange. Hence, this exchange is "good" according to the neoclassical framework, because it is mutually beneficial.

Under a number of very restrictive conditions, it can be shown that a laissez-faire economy maximizes the number of such mutually beneficial exchanges; hence, the neoclassical framework deems laissez-faire capitalism the "best" economic system and considers most government interventions "bad." For example, if the government were to impose a minimum wage of $6.50/hour, then the firm mentioned above would choose not to hire Joe because it is only willing to pay Joe $6/hour. Because the minimum wage policy prevents a mutually beneficial exchange from taking place, effectively preventing the firm and Joe from each gaining $1 from the transaction, the minimum wage policy is "bad."

Christians could have all sorts of reasons for opposing minimum wage legislation, but relying on the ethical standard of pareto efficiency is unacceptable, for it is using fallen, autonomous individuals as the reference point for good and evil. According to the neoclassical framework, if person A and person B both perceive that an exchange is good, then it is good and should be encouraged. The fallacy of using this as a standard for economic stewardship becomes obvious when we consider that the exchange of cocaine is one that both parties consider to be a mutually beneficial transaction. Clearly, if Christ has claimed every square inch of the universe as his own, then he must be the standard by which societies consider how best to allocate their resources. This does not give us all the answers, but it does give us a different starting point.[4]

Some evangelicals might object to all of the above on the grounds that they have biblical arguments in favor of laissez-faire capitalism. Perhaps, but in my own experience the statement of economist Ken Elzinga generally rings true: "The problem in formulating a Christian view of the economic order is not so much the ideology we bring to our economics but rather the ideology we bring to our [biblical] hermeneutics."[5] Too often, Christians, myself included, have been hypnotized by our participation in Western capitalism, making us blind to the presuppositions that we bring to Scripture.

Toward a Holistic Approach

As mentioned above, there is a growing recognition that a comprehensive approach to the problems of the Two-

Thirds World is necessary if real change is to be accomplished and sustained. Such an approach requires Christians to address the effects of sin at all levels, from the international economic order, to the policies of governments in the Two-Thirds World, to the formal and informal institutions of local cultures, down to the worldviews of the poor themselves. It is not just the West that needs to be awakened from its hypnosis. Rather, a comprehensive effort is needed in which the agents and institutions in numerous spheres are fully awake and respond faithfully to their God-given tasks.

Specifically, given the evidence that "trickle-down" does not work without intentional efforts at a micro level and that many of the problems of the poor are spiritual in nature, there is a need for grassroots, faith-based efforts to complement the macroeconomic efforts that Goudzwaard has suggested. Herein lies an opportunity for Christians to embody the shalom of Christ, demonstrating through words and deeds an alternative paradigm for economic life that the world cannot devise on its own.

How can this happen? If growth is to "trickle-down" to the poor, deliberate actions must be taken to ensure that the poor have greater ownership of the factors of production, i.e., land, labor, or capital. This is easier said than done, but microenterprise development (MED), a methodology that provides relatively low-interest loans and vehicles for savings to low-income entrepreneurs, has proven highly effective at increasing the quantity of capital owned by the poor. As a result, numerous Christian relief and development agencies are utilizing MED in their programs across the Two-Thirds World. When combined with evangelism and discipleship, MED programs can be a powerful force for transforming individuals and communities.

Unfortunately, too often Christian MED programs do not look much different from those run by "secular" agencies. Because funding for Christian MED programs comes largely from government sources, such programs are hindered from addressing the spiritual needs of the poor. And without addressing the fundamental religious drives of communities such as Romita's, true and lasting transformation cannot happen. Christian relief and development agencies need to look for creative ways to package their funding from various sources and to partner with local mission agencies and churches in the Two-Thirds World so that together they might model Christ's healing of both the physical and spiritual dimensions of reality. Such cooperation is happening in a few contexts, but there is a need for more and better cases of this partnering so that Christians worldwide can be empowered to embody the fullness of Christ, who ministered in word and deed to the whole person.

The reader might note the similarities between the challenges facing faith-based organizations in the Two-Thirds World and those operating in the United States. In both settings, there is a need for a comprehensive approach in which governments, the business community, and faith-based organizations respect each other's roles and work together without undermining the integrity of their God-given natures and tasks. In short, Kuyper's notion of sphere sovereignty is as relevant for awakening the entire world today as it was a century ago.

A Ten-Trillion-Dollar Stewardship

Response by Larry Reed

"Follow the money," advised the secretive Deep Throat to Watergate investigators Bob Woodward and Carl Bernstein. The money trail led them to the people involved in the cover-up of the Watergate burglary and showed them just how far President Nixon's henchmen would go to get him reelected.

Following the money is also a good idea when looking at how our current global economic system works, who it helps, who it destroys, and who pays to keep it going. If we

Larry Reed is the managing director of the OPPORTUNITY International Network, an association of Christian micro credit organizations providing loans and training to over two hundred thousand clients in thirty-one countries. Larry has also served as Opportunity's Regional Director for Africa, living with his wife and three children for five years in Harare, Zimbabwe. He is a graduate of Wheaton College and the Kennedy School of Government at Harvard University. He is the coeditor of *Serving with the Poor in Africa* and a contributing author to the *Harvard International Review, The Journal of MicroFinance,* and *The New World of Microenterprise Finance.*

are going to wake up and overcome the hypnosis of our age, we need to learn how to follow the money in order to extend God's stewardship to all the places that money touches. If we track where money comes from and where it goes, we will see that we as Christians are not just observers and critics of our current economic system. In fact, we are major players in it and are among those who helped create it. Christians today earn about one-quarter of all the income in the world.[1] Thus, any effort to correct the ills of our current system must begin with a look at how we acquire this income and how we use it.

I very much appreciate Bob Goudzwaard's wake-up call. His perceptive and balanced review of our current global system has challenged me to think again about my own role in that system and how we as Christians should respond to it. In this response, I would like to review and expand on three of the points raised in his lecture: (1) Our international system of economics, information, and communication produces both good and bad results; (2) our stewardship responsibilities extend to the spheres of finance and economics; and (3) change must begin by overcoming our sense of powerlessness and rethinking our deeply held theological views about our place in the market. I would like to conclude, as Goudzwaard did, by suggesting some practical steps we can take to begin to set things right.

The Good, the Bad, the Beautiful, and the Ugly

I work for Opportunity International, a Christian economic development organization that focuses on providing the poor of the developing world with the means to support themselves and their families. From this vantage point I have seen the very good things that our international systems of economics, trade, and communications create, as well as the very bad.

I lived in Zimbabwe from 1991 to 1996. I remember coming back one time to the United States and going to a series of meetings in the Chicago area. As I drove through urban and suburban neighborhoods filled with warm, comfortable, secure homes occupied by middle-class working people, I thought to myself, *There must be something incredibly good with a system that can produce so much wealth for so many people.*

Then I went to the shopping mall and was overwhelmed with not only the choice and selection but also the inanity of so many of the products in the market. I thought, *There must be something twisted with a system in which people can spend so much of their time acquiring things that have so little purpose.*

When I returned to Africa, I saw again the ugly side of this international system. I saw people who had been employed all their adult lives now out on the streets because commodity prices fell and the mining businesses could no longer compete internationally. I saw the World Bank and the International Monetary Fund usher in an economic structural adjustment program. In a few years the cost of the staple foods consumed by the poor doubled, while free trade cut in half the cost of imported items, such as cars and electronics, that only the rich could afford. I saw AIDS spread throughout the country, carried by unemployed young men proving their manhood with sexual conquests and unemployed young women feeding their children by renting out their bodies. I thought, *There has to be something horribly wrong with a system that can perpetuate so much suffering.*

On the other hand, I saw the positive impact Opportunity International could have when we applied good economic principles and Christian values to our work with the poor. Opportunity works through microenterprise lending, so I assisted local leaders to establish a lending institution named Zambuko Trust, which would make loans to people so poor that the banks would not even let them in their doors. We relied on character rather than fixed assets for our collateral. We made loans as small as $50 to help clients purchase sewing machines, buy raw materials, or stock their neighborhood stores. Our clients repaid their loans (we have a 95 percent repayment rate), expanded their businesses, and increased their profits. The interest they paid covered the costs of delivering the credit. The impact did not end there. Clients invested their increased profits in education for their children, and better nutrition, housing, and health care for the entire family. They increased their giving to churches and opened their homes to extended family members who were unemployed. Growing businesses led to improved quality of life and growth in the church.[2]

I had a unique point of view watching this take place. I knew the people in the United States who had given from their abundance to help those who were struggling in another part of the world. I then saw our borrowers in Zimbabwe use this money to increase their income so that they could use their newfound abundance to help others in greater need. As I watched the loans recycle, as I saw this circle of compassion repeat itself again and again, I thought, *There must be something beautiful in a system that not only produces wealth but can also encourage people to use that wealth to extend caring around the world.*

Of course, good and beautiful results generated every so often don't make this a good system. Zambuko Trust now serves 15,000 clients a year, but there are over 2 million unemployed people in Zimbabwe. Around the world, Opportunity International served 175,000 clients last year, while the MicroCredit Summit estimates that there are at least 100 million unemployed or underemployed people who could make good use of loans of this type.[3]

Our global economic system has proven itself capable of creating incredible wealth. This has enabled more people than ever before in human history to live in comfort and material security. However, these fortunate ones still represent only a small percentage of the world's population. The system feeds upon itself, surviving and growing by taking back from people the money it has placed in their hands, enticing them to buy more goods and services, increasingly exotic and unnecessary. How should a Christian called to serve "the least of these brothers of mine" respond to a system that still leaves 1.2 billion people living on less than $1 per day?[4] We should respond by applying the biblical concept of stewardship.

Stewardship of What We Keep, Stewardship of What We Spend

Goudzwaard writes that in a world dominated by the market, competition will become the primary means of human interaction, and the phrase "more is always better than less" will become the mantra. This leads to the imprisonment of the human spirit. Thus, he says, "Our civilization has arrived at a new crossroads of conflicting religious drives."

Of course, this is not the first time in human history that people have been consumed by competition and the desire for more. Those values have driven tyrants throughout the ages, from Nebuchadnezzar to Alexander the Great to Marie Antoinette. Through most of human history the desire for more has consumed the wealthy and powerful. What is unusual in our age is that those values have been adopted by the Western middle class as they, too, have become wealthy and powerful.

The biblical response to wealth and power is the concept of stewardship. Those who hold wealth and power, according to Scripture, do so in trust for God and will be called to give an account of how they use them (Ps. 24:1; Matt. 25:14–30). Since God is Lord of all, this stewardship extends over the entire creation, including the natural environment, the marketplace, and the money we have in our IRA accounts.

Unfortunately, you could go to many churches for a month of Sundays and not hear this message of stewardship. More than likely you would hear the principle of stewardship limited to a call to put more in the offering plate.

Re:Generation magazine recently interviewed Dennis Bakke, the chief executive officer of AES, the world's largest private energy producer, on the topic of stewardship. Bakke describes the traditional view taught on Stewardship Sunday in the church and then comments, "Stewardship is not primarily about the money you give away. It's about the part that you keep. How you steward that part that you keep— that's the hard question! That's what we need to talk about more often!"[5] The article then goes on to describe some of the difficult choices the Bakkes have had to make about their lifestyle to keep it consistent with a stewardship that pleases God. The Bakkes have sought accountability from others in their church for the choices they make about finances.

Why is the principle of stewardship so important in our current global market system? Let's go back to the most basic principle of market economics—supply and demand. The marketplace responds to the demands of consumers. Therefore, if Christians in the marketplace demanded those things that are important in the kingdom of God, the marketplace would find a way to provide them. However, as Goudzwaard has pointed out, the marketplace fuels itself by creating demand, using advertising to convince people to purchase goods and services that they weren't even aware they "needed." A belief in an almighty God who calls us to account for how we use God's resources provides a check on our own acquisitiveness. When we lose this belief, we lose our ability to say no to the desires the advertisers awaken within us. On the other hand, if we do see ourselves as stewards over what we keep, making decisions about our purchases and investments according to the values of the kingdom, we could move the market.

Stewardship of Ten Trillion Dollars

Talk about moving the market may seem quixotic to most. What power do we as Christians have against the massive movements of currency around the world and the controlling power of multinational corporations? A quick look at the numbers shows that we should have much more influence than we currently display.

Studies publicized by Ron Sider estimate the total annual income of Christians worldwide at more than $10 trillion.[6] Since I have a little trouble comprehending trillions, let me give you some comparison numbers. First, the total Gross Domestic Product of the United States in 1998 was $7.9 trillion.[7] Second, the total revenues of the top 350 companies in the world combined equals $10 trillion.[8] Thus, the potential economic power of Christians in the world economy is equivalent to that of the entire U.S. economy, or to the largest 350 companies in the world combined. In fact, the Gross Domestic Product of the world as a whole comes to $40 trillion,[9] so the income of Christians represents one-quarter of the world's annual production.

Some of the implications of this startling statistic are the following:

- Far from being casual observers of the global economic system, we are major players in it. It works to meet our demands.
- If we are major players in it, then we are helping to perpetuate the inequities generated by this system. Pogo has described our current situation well: "We have met the enemy and he is us."[10]
- We have the power to make the market react to our values. If the market will respond to the "New Coke Rebellion," it will surely respond to the needs and desires of people representing $10 trillion.

- If the marketplace does not reflect kingdom values, it must be in no small part because those who claim to follow the King do not reflect those values when making purchases and investments in the market.
- God has placed in the hands of his people sufficient wealth to care for those in need and to carry his message of love throughout the earth. The question is whether we will use that wealth as stewards or as self-serving consumers.

Hypnotized into Powerlessness

Goudzwaard writes, "A kind of virtual reality is now under construction in which a religiously deep myth of autonomous, limitless self-aggrandizement drives us into an ever narrower tunnel. Our minds become closed to alternatives because we believe the present course is an economic necessity. . . . A collective hypnosis sets in." It is this belief, that the way things are is the way they have to be, that blinds us to our own power to change the system. If we just thought for a minute about our power and God's power in relation to the economic system, we would recognize our own potential influence, but those who are hypnotized don't think about their actions.

Here are some examples of how the market responds to values:

- Historically, Christians have demonstrated the capability of building an industry out of caring. The best example is our current hospital system. Gunther Risse, in his book *Mending Bodies, Saving Souls*,[11] explains how hospitals began initially as houses of mercy, refuge, and dying run by Christians to care for the poor who could not afford a personal physician. The monastic orders brought many scientific advances to this practice of care. In the United States, hospitals began as a way for Christians to provide inexpensive care for the poor. Risse's book also points out how modern hospitals have become seduced by technology and economics and have lost the spiritual component of care, a component he considers essential to true healing. A related example is the modern hospice movement, which was started by Christians in response to human suffering and has now become accepted in the medical marketplace.[12]

- Christians helped to develop our current economic system, and therefore, they should be able to help change it. Almost a century ago, Henry P. Crowell and Asa G. Candler developed modern marketing and branding methods by creating the first worldwide brands, Quaker Oats (Crowell) and Coca Cola (Candler). Both were devout Christians who saw themselves as stewards in business who brought good products to the general public at low cost (Candler believed in the medicinal benefits of Coca Cola). Both also donated heavily to Christian causes, especially Christian education.[13] Crowell used his power and wealth to create a committee of business people who fought against public and private corruption in the city of Chicago.[14]

- The current popularity of Cause Related Marketing demonstrates the latent desire in consumers to do good while making purchases. American Express first popularized this concept with its Charge Against Hunger campaign, donating money to hunger-related causes each time someone used his or her card. Avon has a similar identification with Breast Cancer Awareness. These campaigns have proven so popular that the president of the advertising firm Saatchi and Saatchi recommends Cause Related Marketing as a way of creating brand identity and loyalty.[15] A 1997 survey found that 76 percent of consumers would prefer a product associated with a good cause if it had the same price as competing products.[16]

The three examples I have cited demonstrate both the ability of Christians to shape the market and the ability of the market to shape the industries and practices developed by Christians. The hospital system developed by Christians through the ages has now become an industry driven by competition and bottom-line thinking. The marketing techniques developed by Crowell and Candler have become the means by which unreal needs are created while real needs go unmet. Cause Related Marketing can become an inoculation against real caring, allowing a person purchasing a $500 bauble to feel good about themselves because $1 of that purchase goes to help the poor.

Battling a foe as strong and seductive as human greed requires constant vigilance, regular systems of accountability, and strong support from a community of shared values.

Going to the Deepest Level within Me

I have been writing about the need for Christians to take more personal responsibility for the economic system in which they earn and spend. In this section I want to follow Goudzwaard's lead by looking at the deepest level, the level of religious conviction about our world and our place in it. I was going to write about the hypocrisy of Christians who say they believe in an all-powerful God and then feel as if they are powerless to change the marketplace. Then I realized that I am one of those people. It is only fair, then, for me to examine myself to see how my deepest-level beliefs affect my actions.

If you compared my Visa statement to my espoused values, I'm afraid you would find little correlation. I say I believe in a God who owns everything and I am God's steward here on earth. I say that God is all powerful and overflowing in abundance, therefore, I don't need to hoard. I say that God has demonstrated his love for me in such a profound way that I should give all my life in service to the work of God on earth. I say that God has a special concern for the poor, and I show my love for God by serving those in need. I say that God is full of joy and wants to make my joy complete.

My Visa and bank statements say that I live comfortably, I eat well, I contribute more than my share to the pollution of the earth with the gasoline I consume in two vehicles, and I am saving up enough to make sure that I can continue my current lifestyle after I stop working. The statements also show that I give away a little more than the average American and I've put more of my savings into socially responsible mutual funds than is typical. But otherwise it would be difficult to look at my spending and investment patterns and detect a set of values that differed from the prevailing values of our culture.

What impedes my progress to living out my stated values?

- I find the task too huge and daunting. I spend too much time at work, I have three teenage children and a wife whom I need to serve, and I have responsibilities to my church and other voluntary organizations. I just don't see where I'm going to find the time to change the world's economic system as well. Even just the work of finding out how to do one small thing right, such as figuring out which companies don't employ sweatshop labor, takes more time than I have available.
- I let one or two movements in the right direction convince me that I am doing enough. I work for a Christian organization, and I could probably make more money if I worked for a profitable business. I tithe my income to my church and other Christian organizations. Isn't that stewardship enough?
- I have few good examples to follow. The Amish and the Bruderhof provide the only real examples of consistent stewardship applied to the marketplace that I know,

and I'm not ready to go that far. Otherwise, I rarely talk about personal finances with people at work or in my small group, so I don't know anyone I could emulate in this area.

- I don't have a system of accountability for my spending. If I don't do my work properly, my board lets me know. If I'm not spending enough time with my family, my wife lets me know. If I don't pay my taxes, the IRS lets me know. But if I spend God's money on frivolous things, no one really knows.

A theologian reading my justifications would probably say I have trouble understanding and applying the concept of the immanence of God. I acknowledge God's existence and lordship, but I do not act as if I know that God is right here, right now, able to work through me in each small choice I make.

Goudzwaard's lecture covered global issues of economics, finance, communication, and information. Why am I writing about my own individual choices? Because our market system of economics is built upon the individual choices of consumers. If we want to change this system, if we want to bend it in the direction of eternal values, then it will be through a series of small individual choices that each of us makes. We cannot change everything all at once, but that should not prevent us from making our next financial decision an act of stewardship.

Measuring What Matters

A lack of good information and an absence of measures that reflect our values complicate our attempts to exercise stewardship in our financial decisions. The packaging of the products we buy tells us their price, their contents, and where they were assembled. It does not tell us if the company that produced it despoils God's creation, exploits its workers, or corrupts officials. The same is true for the statistics we use to measure the success and wealth of companies and countries. Measures such as Gross Domestic Product, Net Present Value, and Market Capitalization tell us something about economic value but nothing about lasting value. Robert Kennedy spoke out about this thirty years ago when he said,

> The gross national product does not allow for the health of our children, the quality of their education, or the joy of their play; it does not include the beauty of our poetry or the strength of our marriages, the intelligence of our public debate or the integrity of our public officials. It measures neither our wit nor our courage, neither our wisdom nor our learning, neither our compassion nor our devotion to our country. It measures everything, in short, except that which makes life worthwhile, and it can tell us everything about America except why we are proud that we are Americans.[17]

Fortunately, the world of measures and statistics is not static. Every measurement is an abstraction that simplifies the world in order to make comparisons. Economists and business people constantly tinker with the measures they use to incorporate a wider range of data. Recently this has led to a spate of new indicators that do more to measure a company's impact on people and their environment.

Goudzwaard recommends the development of the category of "Publicly Authorized Company" for those companies that receive positive recommendations from the environmental, labor, consumer, and civil society communities. David Korten recommends a more rigorous audit, which he calls a Market Efficiency Audit. This audit would measure the external impact of a company, both good and bad, and compare it to the profits a company generates.[18] The Council for Economic Priorities grades the social responsibility of corporations in seven categories and publishes its findings in the book *Shopping for a Better World*.[19] Simon Zadek of the New Economics Foundation in Britain has worked with

Richard Evans of Tradecraft, a company that imports products from the developing world, to develop a social audit system based on the ideas of George Goyder.[20] The Body Shop and other corporations in the United Kingdom are now employing this system. The Body Shop has also turned over the responsibility for this social auditing to its auditors, KPMG, so that they can use the tools to audit other companies.[21]

The social audit work by Zadek and Evans provides a classic example of the marketplace responding to people who value ethical behavior. If consumers demand to know more about the ethical and business practices of the companies they buy from, those companies with nothing to hide will find an economic advantage in letting consumers know about their good practices. They will find ways of getting reliable and easily understood information to those consumers. At the same time, audit companies will recognize the potential for a new source of revenue and will develop the tools and skills needed to carry out these social audits.

Moving from Talk to Action

The specific actions we decide to take as stewards in the international marketplace are up to each of us. We will need to use our education, skills, and creativity to apply biblical principles where we have seldom applied them before. Below I offer a few suggestions to get the ball rolling. Since most of the discussion in this book is about how multinational corporations must change and what governments should do to police them, I will focus most heavily on suggestions for how change can begin at the level of individuals, families, workplaces, and churches.

Individuals and Families

The *New York Times* has estimated that, on average, we each receive thirty-five hundred advertising messages every day.[22] If we do not develop any countervailing source of information, we will eventually believe that our lives cannot be fulfilled until we purchase the products being advertised. Taking time for reflection and developing habits that feed the soul form the first line of defense. Here are some other suggestions:

- Take some time to learn more about the products on which you spend the most money. Where and how are they produced? What raw materials are used in their production? What impact does the making of these products have on our environment? What sort of ethical track record do the companies have that produce these products? What sort of labor practices do they have? *Shopping for a Better World* provides a good starting point for this research.
- Take time to learn about and pray for one developing country. What is the average income? How many are unemployed? What sort of goods does the country produce? What are the physical and spiritual needs of its people? What foreign companies operate there, and what sort of impact do they have?
- Develop a set of questions to think through when making decisions about purchases and investments. What of lasting value will come out of this decision? How will this purchase or investment bless others? Fifty years from now (if I'm still alive), will I be happy I made this choice? Ten thousand years from now (in eternity), will I be happy I made this choice?
- Develop one or more nonfinancial investment goals such as, by the time I retire I would like to have created five hundred jobs, or sent five hundred children to school, or paid for the construction of fifty churches, and so on.
- Examine the holdings of your mutual fund(s) to see if the companies you have invested in reflect your val-

ues. If not, look into investments in socially responsible mutual funds.[23]

Workplaces

Spirituality has become a popular topic in the corporate halls of Western businesses. Here's a quote from the August 1998 edition of *Fast Company* magazine:

> For consultants, spirituality in the workplace has become a growth stock. Almost anything can qualify, from a Bible-study lunch group to a generic goal-setting program that starts with a mission statement and seeks to connect personal purpose to actual work. . . . The simple fact is, more and more people at more and more companies are flocking to any program that helps them connect what they do for the bottom line to what they value most deeply.[24]

Christians in the workplace should help their companies build these connections. We should find other workers who share our values and organize discussions that help the company examine its practices and influence according to spiritual values.

Churches

The church can play a critical role in providing ground-level training in how to demonstrate stewardship in the marketplace. Some ways churches can do this include the following:

- Hold classes on the stewardship theme and then study our current economic system and the teachings of Scripture that relate to it. (My church, LaSalle Street Church in Chicago, just completed a forum series on this topic.)

- Study the examples of business leaders and workers in the past who have demonstrated good stewardship.
- Invite members to discuss ways in which they seek to demonstrate stewardship in their marketplace decisions.
- Have members of the congregation study various industries and then give reports on what to consider when purchasing those products.
- Provide lists of companies in the area with proven track records of good ethical behavior.
- Invite the CEOs of major corporations in town to come to church and discuss the impact, ethics, and values of their companies.
- Organize small groups of those willing to be accountable to each other in the area of their financial choices, sharing their kingdom goals and their financial statements.

Other Levels

From our own actions as individuals in the market, in the workplace, and in church there should flow coordinated action as responsible citizens. We should pressure our government for policies that encourage real production and discourage speculation, such as a tax code that taxes speculative gains at a higher rate than gains from longer-term investments.

We should seek to apply economic solutions to the ravages caused by currency speculation in the international arena. The International Monetary Fund and the U.S. Treasury both have funds of over $40 billion used to rescue countries whose currencies face rapid devaluation. Many times the needs of the poor get overlooked in the way these funds are applied. The oversight of these funds by Congress and the directors of the IMF should include a review of whether the currency intervention takes place in a way that benefits the poor. A bill currently before Congress, the Microenterprise for Self Reliance Act, calls for the establishment of a similar type of fund for financial institutions that lend to the poor.

A similar argument holds for the debt relief promoted by the Jubilee 2000 movement. In many developing countries debt relief will be necessary to promote economic growth and social equity. However, debt relief should be tied to tangible improvements in health care, education, and economic opportunity for the poor. Otherwise it could become the means of allowing corrupt governments to buy more weapons or stash more money abroad.

We should also explore ways to direct the enormous flows of international capital into productive enterprises that employ the poor and build societies. For example, it will take $20 billion of investment to provide loans to 100 million poor families. While this number seems huge, it pales in comparison to the wealth in the global community. This $20 billion represents only two-tenths of 1 percent of the annual income of Christians. By investing a very small percentage of their income in loans to the poor, Christians could provide a stable income for 100 million families and have a direct impact on over 1 billion people.

A Small Application

In my work with Opportunity International, foreign exchange rates and inflation often wreak havoc on our attempts to serve the poor. In order for Opportunity to have the ability to serve a large proportion of the number of poor people who could utilize the credit we offer, we need to find some ways of mitigating the negative consequences of foreign currency speculation.

In our work we have learned how to make lending to the poor profitable. Our lending institutions can earn enough from the interest they charge on their loans to cover all their costs, including the cost of the capital they employ. This means that they should be able to attract commercial investment, which would allow them to reach hundreds of thousands more people than they can reach with donated funds. However, if an investor in the United States would like to have her money used on behalf of the poor but would like to have that money back at some later date, then we have to contend with foreign exchange risk. If the local currency plummets during the time one of our lending institutions is borrowing money, then the lending institution will never be able to earn enough in local currency to repay the loan. What we need in Opportunity are Christian investors who will be willing to bear the foreign exchange risk on behalf of the poor. This money could be placed in a pool, and, with a good investment manager, could be used to balance out foreign exchange rate losses. This would leverage much more money that could be used as loans to the poor and would help create jobs, strengthen families, and build communities. A fund of $5 million could leverage $20 million in capital for the poor. Over a five-year period of time this fund could create or sustain jobs for 500,000 people living in poverty.

The Attractiveness of a God Who Rules over All

If we could follow the money of Christians, if we could trace the $10 trillion to see how it was earned and where it goes, what would we find? Would we be able to say that Christians are exercising stewardship over this money, earning, spending, and investing in ways that store up eternal treasures? Or would we say that Christians have also fallen under the hypnosis of our age, feeling powerless against the marketplace and not seeing the relevance of their own economic choices to their role in God's kingdom?

A consistent Christian worldview has economic implications. In fact, one of the most attractive aspects of Christianity is its relevance to all areas of life. Christianity has grown most quickly when it has demonstrated its full impact on life and culture. In the first two centuries after Christ, the Christian message of the equality of all people in the eyes of God came as liberating good news to women and servants. They, in turn, spread this good news to the children of the household and then eventually to the fathers. It entered into the household of the Roman Emperor Constantine in this way, and so became the state religion of Rome. At that point, though, Christianity became indistinguishable from Roman culture, lost its ability to confront the state and society, and lost much of its attractiveness.[25]

The situation today is no different. Where Christianity has a clear impact on all areas of life, it grows quickly. I saw this in Africa, where those who became Christians and joined a church also changed their lifestyles. More money went to the household and less to alcohol and illicit relationships. New Christians shared more of their wealth and time with others. They also gained a wide network of friends who would support them when they faced rough times. Every aspect of their lives, spiritual, political, economic, and social, underwent transformation because of the application of the gospel. This has fueled the growth of the church in Africa, as it has in Latin America and South Korea.

In the West, however, the market has co-opted Christianity in much the same way that Constantine co-opted the church. Christians have become indistinguishable from any other buyers and sellers in the marketplace, and so our message has become increasingly irrelevant. Two recent magazine articles demonstrate this irrelevance. The first is the millennium edition of the *Economist,* which closes with an obituary for God. The subheading to the article reads, "After a lengthy career, the Almighty recently passed into history. Or did he?"[26]

The second is the January edition of *Civilization* magazine, which has a cover story on the "Buddha Boom." It describes the rapid rise of Buddhism in the United States, from about 200,000 adherents in 1960 to over 2 million today. Jan Nattier writes that one reason for Buddhism's growing attraction is that it offers a consistent set of ideals and practices that helps its followers operate with spiritual values in our modern market economy.[27]

The kingdom of this world is ruled by scarcity and death. In such a world, greed and self-aggrandizement have become driving forces. Yet all of us sense within us the presence of another kingdom, an eternal kingdom swelling with abundance, a kingdom ruled by the love of its Creator. This eternal kingdom broke into our world most tangibly in the person of Jesus Christ. Based on his example, we who follow him know that we can begin living now the type of life that we will live for eternity. We can let the values of the eternal kingdom guide our choices in all realms of life, including our spending and investing. We can make those choices with the security of knowing that we are loved by our God, the original Creator who has never lost the ability to make more.

We need not fear "the great and powerful market," for the market responds to us. Like Dorothy in Oz, we need to peer behind the curtain and recognize that the principal power the market has is our fear of it. Otherwise it must be our servant, responding to our values and desires. If we wake up and see the market for what it really is, a tool that must come under the stewardship of Christ, then we will realize that God has already given us the power to make the changes we desire.

A New Agenda for Economic Theory

Response by Adolfo García de la Sienra

The Challenge of Evolutionism

Bob Goudzwaard begins by quoting Abraham Kuyper's opening statement in a speech given on October 20, 1899: "Our nineteenth century is dying away under the hypnosis of the dogma of Evolution." Goudzwaard judges that, given the complexity of our own age with its multiplicity of idols and spirits, it may be better for us, one hundred years later, first to give careful attention to the factual processes before us.

There can be no doubt that our age is far more complex than Kuyper's, but it is also clear that the dogma of evolu-

Adolfo García de la Sienra is professor of economic philosophy at the University of Veracruz, Mexico. He earned his Ph.D. at Stanford University and has taught at the University of Mexico. An author of numerous articles in Spanish and English in both technical and general subjects, he has lectured abroad and is a member of the International Association of Reformed Philosophy. This response was written with support of Conacyt Project 28630H.

tion is still strong today, especially in the field of economics, where it has given rise to a whole new theory, the so-called evolutionary economics. This theory tries to explain economic change by means of biological analogies such as genetic variation (technological innovation) and natural selection (market selection). The intent is to understand the economy as something determined by the survival of the fittest, the fittest being those firms that are able to choose successful routines (technologies, marketing and managerial procedures, and so forth). There is indeed much about current economic life that gives it the appearance of a merciless struggle for survival. However, even hard-core evolutionary economists have had to admit that the economic jungle, in contrast to the biotic one, needs an institutional setting that cannot be built and sustained purely by means of ferocious competitive behavior. Successful economies require cooperation, normativity, and many other forms of human behavior.

Nevertheless, the dogma of evolution, in the form of an economic ideology that is used more to legitimize than to explain the current chaos in financial markets, is as strong as ever. The quest for monetary profit for its own sake has begun to overrule any other consideration in the economy and to encroach on other spheres of life as well. If this continues, the so-called traditional forms of human interaction and communication will be reduced to essentially economic or financial transactions that know of no other value than profit-in-order-to-get-more-profit.

Goudzwaard warns that consumer preferences can no longer be considered static or an expression of the autonomy of the consumer. On the contrary, preferences can be influenced and altered in many ways, and they are no longer exercised merely in relation to consumer goods at stores like Wal-Mart. Today, even human values are considered to be nothing more than preferences and thus subject to market forces. Previous regulations or a sense of decency may once have restrained radio and television advertising, for example, but today even that is changing. Goudzwaard calls our attention to the Internet's seemingly limitless power to intrude into the lives of families and individuals.

Hence, I believe the dogma of evolution has found in economic competition its Trojan Horse by which to penetrate the heart of culture and all of society with its worldview—its religious drive and interpretation of reality. What a remarkable way to preach a religious message, namely, to force economic competition on men and women the world over, as if it were a natural necessity.

As I understand him, Goudzwaard is elucidating two major contemporary problems: (1) the increasing power of global financial markets, and (2) the impact of competition on the structure of entire societies. Goudzwaard finds the religious root of these problems in the modern tendency to make market competition the universal law of all of society. This tendency is based on the assumptions that human appetites are insatiable and that economic rules represent unchangeable laws. All of this is pure evolutionism, grounded in a deep religious dialectic expressed in the drive for human autonomy in a world believed to be governed by natural necessity. Understanding and exposing evolutionism for what it is, namely, an expression of modern humanism, should, in my opinion, be placed high on the agenda for reformational Christian philosophers. But we must also take up the task of constructing an economic theory, along reformational lines, free from humanist presuppositions. Toward that end and in the spirit of Goudzwaard's analysis of the global economy, my aim in what follows is to outline an agenda for Christian economists and philosophers of economics.

Economics as a Natural Science

According to the old scholastic doctrines, economics entails both normative and natural laws. Economics is an uncertain and imprecise science that deals with human behavior. Human behavior was understood not as blind and mechanical but as obeying moral standards as well as laws of nature. This view of economic life was replaced during the sixteenth, seventeenth, and eighteenth centuries by a new doctrine based on the new humanistic science ideal. Human responsibility, as bound by certain standards of moral conduct, was no longer considered relevant to economic science. The economy came to be understood as a natural process ruled entirely by natural laws, very much like physical processes were governed by physical laws.[1] A century or two before the rise of evolutionary economics, early modern economic theory was built on the analogy of physical energy.[2]

George Soros still thinks that the prevailing doctrine in economics today, of which he is critical, is equilibrium theory, which is built on the analogy of physical energy. He complains, however, that such a conception, as well as the market ideology it supports, is subverted by a fundamental and unsolvable problem: "Unlike those [events] that concern the physicists and the chemists, social and economic events presuppose the presence of thinking agents. And thinking agents can change the rules of the economy and social systems by virtue of their own ideas about such rules."[3]

Soros's remark is somewhat unfair to current equilibrium theory, which tries to take into account uncertainty, imperfect information, and strategic behavior by reflective agents. Nevertheless, it is interesting to see one of the fittest survivors in the global financial jungle rejecting the idea that the rules of economics are abiding and immutable. Soros claims that economic science cannot be developed along the lines of physical science, with its concept of equilibrium, as classical economists thought. Being the good humanist that he is, however, he continues to be occupied with the quest for human autonomy[4] (and making money). With this as his highest indisputable value, he remains blind to trans-subjective, supra-arbitrary standards or norms for human behavior. Human happiness, in his view, must be measured by the degree to which humans become more autonomous and self-sufficient. In the absence of an objective criterion by which economic excesses and mistakes can be corrected in an open society, the economist must be satisfied with aggregating all the subjective choices and judgments individuals make in order to obtain a criterion of social choice considered binding for everyone. In other words, for Soros, as for most economists, any norms or standards appropriate to guide social choice must arise from autonomous individuals, subjectively, not from God and the good creation order.

Reasoning in this way, Soros displays one of the illnesses that afflicts contemporary economic liberalism in both its energistic and evolutionary camps. Liberal humanists are compelled to make social choices, even though they may be blind to the normative structure of the world. Consequently, they need some way to derive from human autonomy itself the criterion for making such choices. Within their framework of individualistic assumptions and autonomous human choices, they believe that such a criterion can be found by means of aggregating all the individual, arbitrary rankings of social states (circumstances, conditions, etc.). However, as Kenneth Arrow has shown,[5] this is impossible. Complete individual freedom and arbitrariness in matters of social choice are no more possible than social well-being in a democratic society that lacks a degree of consensus on the ends of society. And from a Christian point of view, even a social consensus is unacceptable as a standard for evaluating social welfare. The individuals who belong to a society, as well as their consensus, may be corrupt. The recognition of this fact lies behind Goudzwaard's relentless criticism of the idea of "the autonomy of the consumer." Goudzwaard's concern in this respect should be understood as a warning that not just any consensus about what makes for a good society—not even a unanimous consensus—is useful for a reformational approach to economic justice or for the construction of economic theory.

Toward a Normative Economics

In opposition to current economics, I would like to point toward an economic theory in which human behavior is not understood as blind and mechanical but as obeying moral standards. My proposal is to formulate this in terms of a social-welfare criterion that accords with God's norms for creation.

Suppose that we want to choose a system of needs that is sustainable, fair, and respects the environment. A "system of needs," in economic terms, is a specified production-consumption pattern that is reproducible in the following sense: At the beginning of a period, society has a certain stock of commodities, several technological possibilities, and a labor force with given skills. Society chooses (by certain means) a production process that employs the labor force in a certain way, consumes certain inputs, and yields a given output. If the newly obtained output "resets" the economy to repeat a similar process, we say that the system of needs is reproducible. The term "system of needs" thus conveys the idea that this is a system in which consumption and production interlock.

Reformational economics repudiates the claim that "the market" (whatever that may be) necessarily chooses a social optimum—a system of needs that maximizes social well-being in accord with creation-order standards. Nothing guarantees, in particular, that mere profit-maximization will eventually lead to such an optimum. It is well known that profit-maximizing producers in a competitive, decentralized economy always choose efficient processes. But it is also clear that this by itself does not guarantee that they will choose processes that are acceptable from other points of view. For instance, the imposition of a rate of consumption over a certain length of time can be destructive of precious traditions and cultural traits, as well as of the environment. This is the reason why Goudzwaard has always insisted that global decision making in the economy at large must not be made on the basis of pure profit. What is required is a democratic system in which social choices are made in a way that acknowledges and accords with supra-arbitrary norms.

How could a scheme like the one that has been sketched above be used to evaluate the globalization process and propose rules for the same? Let me suggest in broad strokes how this might be done.

Goudzwaard has pointed out that the new form of exploitation known as neoliberalism and globalization is characterized by a fast and unimpeded flow of financial capital around the world, but, above all, as he correctly stresses, by a lack of correspondence between the real sphere and the financial sphere of the international economy. He remarks that only 5 percent of the international money transfers occur for the purpose of buying and selling goods and services in the real sphere.

This suggests that the prevalent prices in the international markets are not the "real ones," but such a consideration brings us back to a very ancient problem, namely, the problem of value. One way of attacking this problem within a framework such as the one sketched above is to define the "real" prices of goods and services as those that result from the establishment and maintenance of a system of needs that accords with creation-order criteria of social well-being. These prices would measure in units of obedience the economic value of goods and services! If social welfare in this framework is really democratic and obedient, then prices wildly deviating from the "real" ones would have to be considered perverse. The problem would remain of designing the proper policies to enforce the correct prices (it is obvious that the fetish of unbridled "markets" should leave us unimpressed). Arriving at such policies should be the result of international cooperation and should be reflected in international law.

It seems to me that an economic agenda such as this one does away with evolutionism, mechanicism, and irresponsibility. It returns to the hands of an awakened and responsible humanity the reins of a process that now appears to have gone awry. It seems to me that to deal seriously with the problems involved in constructing an adequate criterion for social welfare, and to do so both locally and globally, is a way of answering the great challenge that Goudzwaard has posed to all Christian economists and philosophers.

A Note for Economists on Arrow's General Possibility Theorem

Imagine that we could describe all the possible conditions and circumstances ("states") of a society with a set of "social states" or alternatives S. This set—called the *environment*—contains as members "complete descriptions" of all the possible social states. According to Kenneth J. Arrow, founding father of this field,

> The most precise definition of a social state would be a complete description of the amount of each commodity in the hands of each individual, the amount of labor to be supplied by each individual, the amount of each productive resource invested in each type of productive activity, and the amounts of various types of collective activity, such as municipal ser vices, diplomacy and its continuation by other means, and the erection of statues of famous men.[6]

Suppose now that there is a number n of individuals in society, each having a peculiar conception of how society should be structured and each one willing to have some particular social state enforced. Imagine also that you, individual i among these n individuals, are asked to rank the elements of S, ranking them from the one that is most acceptable to you down to the one you find least acceptable, given your values and beliefs about what a good society must be, so that you end up with a relation (call it "preference") that stipulates, for every pair of states x and y, which of x or y is more acceptable to you. If your values make you find x no worse than y, write "xR_iy"; if you find x as good as y, write "xI_iy"; and if you find x strictly better than y write "xP_iy." Your ranking is required to be *complete* or *connected* in the sense that for any two possible options x and y, your ranking stipulates that precisely one of the three relationships xP_iy, yP_ix, or xI_iy holds. Your ranking is also required to be *transitive*, in the sense that xR_iz whenever xR_iy and yR_iz. Let $C(S)$ be the set of all alternatives chosen in S; we require that it be the set of all alternatives that are most preferred, so that $C(S)$ contains those alternatives x such that xR_iy for every y in S. This means that you choose precisely those alternatives that are the most preferred ones. The solution to the problem of social choice we would be seeking with this kind of formula requires the existence of a *social welfare function* (swf), i.e., a process or rule f, which, for each set of individual orderings $R_1, \ldots, R_n$, states a corresponding social ordering of alternative social states, $R = f(\{R_i\})$. This rule or process is supposed to "induce" a social ordering out of the rankings of the individuals.

A universal swf would be one that is applicable to any community or to any given set of individual orderings. There is no such universal rule, but there are many ways of specifying conditions over the individual orderings that guarantee the existence of a corresponding swf. An *admissible* set of individual orderings is one for which a corresponding swf exists. The humanist idea of autonomy imposes certain conditions on the individual orderings, notably that they must be generated in a manner entirely free from any tradition, sacred code, external norm, or a previous agreement regarding the existence of a social order binding on everyone. The question is whether a set of individual orderings satisfying these conditions is admissible. The answer to the question is no, but it is important for Christian economists to see precisely what is at fault in the conditions defining the liberal conception of individual orderings. It seems to me that at least some important and fundamental aspects of a reformational agenda for economic theory can arise out of a criticism of such conditions from a creation-order point of view.

The first condition gives expression to the idea that a truly free individual does not in principle have to admit to any external restrictions on his conception of social life. This means that any particular individual's ordering of social states is acceptable in principle. Thus, individual $_i$ at some time may have an ordering R_i in which, for instance, marriage is highly ranked, but at another time (or another individual) may have an ordering in which marriage is despised. This condition, which is a curious formulation of the leveling of social structures that is so typical of liberalism, is called the unrestricted domain condition (U) and can be formulated as follows. Condition U: The domain of the social welfare function f includes all logically possible n-tuples of orderings of S.

The second condition—I, the independence of irrelevant alternatives—is a very reasonable and innocuous one, namely, that in a given choice situation only the relevant alternatives be taken into account, so that a restriction of the original set of alternatives to a smaller one should not affect the original orderings. An economic example is that if you are considering buying ice cream and go to the shop thinking that you prefer chocolate to vanilla and vanilla to strawberry, but you find that there is no vanilla, then you still prefer chocolate to strawberry. Condition I: As long as the individual preferences remain the same over a subset S' of S, the social choice from S' must remain the same.

The third condition, called the weak Pareto principle, P, is required to make the swf really sensitive to changes in the individual orderings. It is self-explanatory and entirely acceptable. Condition P: If everybody strictly prefers x to y, then xPy; i.e., the social welfare function chooses x over y.

The final condition is also acceptable. It is a condition that requires that the swf be democratically established and not the result of the imposition by some dictator. In other words, there is no individual or pair of alternatives such that everybody must agree with the ranking that that individual makes of these alternatives. Condition D: There is no individual i such that, for all individual orderings $\{R_j\}$, and pairs of alternatives x, y, xP_iy implies xRy.

The following General Possibility Theorem is an astonishing result, achieved originally by Arrow[7] (the proof is omitted):

Theorem 1: If there are more than three individuals, then there is no social welfare function satisfying simultaneously conditions U, I, P, and D. This theorem, which can be compared in depth and conclusiveness to Kurt Gödel's Incompleteness Theorem, establishes once and for all that even in a pure democracy not anything goes. Indeed, if we accept conditions I, P, and D, which are not problematic, we find that the problem is in condition U. Hence, not all logically possible individual orderings are feasible. Complete arbitrariness in matters of social choice is thus ruled out. Even a democratic swf is impossible unless there is a certain social consensus on the ends of society. The problem, from a Christian point of view, is that even such a consensus may be "perverse," and thus, having a consensus and a corresponding swf can be very unsatisfactory. Historicism has always argued that a consensus does not require abiding supra-arbitrary social norms but arises naturally from the *Volksgeist*. But from a Christian perspective, the so-called *Volksgeist* (i.e., the prevalent *mores* in a given society) is entirely unacceptable as a standard for producing a good swf: The individuals belonging to a society, as well as their consensus, may be corrupt.

Thus, the kind of swf that is required for a reformational economic theory is not one resulting from just any consensus but one resulting from a consensus of the right sort. Such a consensus need not be unanimous, because there is no unanimity even within the confines of the Reformed Christian community, let alone the entire (universal) Christian church. Therefore, the question that arises now is, What condition should be placed instead of U, in order to get a swf for reformational economics?

In 1951 Arrow wrote that "the correct mathematical generalization of the unanimity condition is not easy to see."[8] In the same book, Arrow had explored a more relaxed unanimity condition proposed by Duncan Black,[9] known as single-peakedness, but Arrow added that "Black's postulate, elegant though it be, is not obviously applicable, though perhaps deeper investigation would change the verdict."[10] As it turns out, this postulate is still considered nowadays, half a century later, to be the one that defines the most important class of restricted domain conditions.[11] It would be interesting to discuss how it could be interpreted and applied to represent individual orderings of social states arising from values held by reformational philosophy. Let me finish this section by discussing how this might be done.

Suppose that you, agent i, are presented again with a set of possible social states S—alternatives—and that you are also given a strict linear ordering of S reflecting the understanding of an "expert" on justice of the meaning-kernel of the juridical modality as applied to S. Let T be this ordering, and let xTy mean that x is fairer than y for the "expert." Now, your sense of justice may be so similar to that of the expert that you find that T is a good representation of your own understanding, so that your own (strict) preference relation P_i coincides with T (i.e., for every pair of alternatives x, y, both xP_iy and xTy). But it is also quite possible that there are discrepancies among these orderings. Since the meaning-kernel of a modality is not a Platonic form, this situation is perfectly possible and is to be expected. Imagine now that the members of a Christian organization (e.g., the constituency of a political party) have a family of orderings (one for each individual) $\{P_i\}$ reflecting their respective understandings of the relative fairness of the alternatives. The single-peakedness condition (SP) consists of the following: that each individual i has a most preferred alternative x_i such that, as the alternatives move away from x_i in any direction, with respect to the ordering T—that of the expert—they become less and less preferred for i. This condition, which is not easy to interpret, yields the following interesting result (the proof is omitted), which may constitute a starting point for discussing the foundations of reformational economics.

Theorem 2: There is a social welfare function that satisfies simultaneously conditions SP, I, P, and D. This function is generated by pairwise majority voting and is connected and transitive. It is clear to me that an important challenge open before us is to propose other weak-unanimity conditions that may be more suitable for obtaining a full-blown swf, democratically constructed, that entirely recognizes the law-structure of this created world.

Conclusion

James W. Skillen

Awakening, Maturation, and Conversion

Bob Goudzwaard exposes a hypnosis of the Western mind that leads people to believe "there is no alternative" (TINA) to the quest for limitless economic and technological growth. He even warns that this hypnotized state may prove to be stronger and more dangerous than the control exercised by national socialism and communism over millions of people. Hypnosis is a dangerous thing if one does not awaken from the trance. Leaving the hypnotized state means regaining conscious control over oneself—becoming responsible again.

Later in his essay, Goudzwaard switches metaphors and urges westerners, especially Christians, to put childishness behind them and to assume the responsibility of adults. The similarity between childishness and the hypnotized state is that the person is subject to the control of another and unable to exercise full responsibility. The difference is that there is nothing abnormal about childishness in a child. A child is not temporarily unconscious but is merely going through a process whereby parents and others bear responsibility to guide the child to maturity at a pace that coincides with the child's bodily, emotional, and mental growth.

What bearing do these two conditions, used as metaphors, have on our understanding of the global economy? How can they help us assess the process of globalization? Before we can answer these questions, we must recall something else that Goudzwaard and his respondents have said or implied. All agree that something deeper than capital flows and economic institutions drives the decisions that people make in the global economy today. There is a religious root or wellspring of life from which arise the deepest human commitments, the strongest aspirations, and the most enduring cultural and social patterns. Goudzwaard wants us to see that the ideology of limitless economic expansion is rooted in a deeper faith in human autonomy that fuels the quest for self-sufficiency and self-aggrandizement. That faith and way of life are fundamentally at odds with the Christian faith and way of life, as all the authors point out. The humanistic commitment to the goal of complete autonomy is, thus, from a Christian perspective, a counter-religion, an expression of idolatrous service to a false god. Consequently, as Brian Fikkert says, if a false religion is the primary dynamic behind international economic developments, then what is needed is conversion to the true God revealed in Christ. Conversion, not a wake-up call, is needed. Turning to the true God from false gods is required, not maturation from childhood to adulthood. Which is it, then? In order to foster the good aspects of globalization and to halt or reform the bad aspects, do people need conversion, or maturation from childishness to adulthood, or a wake-up call? Or do they need all three?

Goudzwaard begins his essay by saying that we need to distinguish at least three different levels of human life. The deepest, all-encompassing level—the religious depth-level—

directs the shaping of culture and society. The cultural patterns and social structures, in turn, determine or influence the events, circumstances, and developments that are most apparent each day. We might ask, therefore, whether the type of human responsibility required at each of these three levels has anything to do with the three calls for "conversion," "maturation," and "awakening" to which the authors refer. Could it be that *conversion* is the appropriate response to error at the religiously deep level, that *maturation* is required at the cultural and social level, where reform must grow from obedient response to the creation-order purposes of the true God, and that *waking up* ought to happen at the level of everyday experience—buying, selling, working, consuming, and investing—where people should become aware that they bear adult responsibility and are not merely subject to the will of others or to the fates?

Bearing Responsibility

Every generation, says Goudzwaard, stands before the face of God. Each generation of human beings bears real responsibility. The question is, Who bears what kind of responsibility? This is perhaps the most important question and challenge arising from the preceding essays. Adolfo García de la Sienra emphasizes that the fundamental error of economic theorists, who depend on physical and evolutionary hypotheses for their science, is that they cannot account for human responsibility—for moral choices. This criticism stands at the heart of Goudzwaard's essay, for he is convinced that people will not awaken from their sense of powerlessness as long as they accept the misunderstanding of themselves as pawns of a market mechanism that inevitably determines the course of globalization. Larry Reed says that Christians will act like everyone else until they realize that they can and should make different choices in the way they spend and invest their $10 trillion in the global economy.

Yet who are the responsible actors that our authors are addressing? Surely the millions of Christians around the world who control $10 trillion do not constitute an acting body. They are not organized in a way that would allow them to decide by majority vote or consensus how to reorient all $10 trillion of their spending and investment. No, they are organized in millions of different families, in countless places of employment, in thousands of different churches, in more than a hundred different political systems, and they invest in thousands of different companies through dozens of different stock markets. Consequently, even if individual Christians have begun to turn their hearts from false gods to the true God, their obedience—their full conversion—to God in all areas of life requires that they seek reform, where needed, in specific institutions and cultural patterns where they bear responsibility. Bank owners and governments must act to change banking laws and bank behaviors. Corporate managers and stock holders bear responsibility to reorient corporate goals and behaviors. Government officials and lawmakers must make public-legal decisions—deciding whether to forgive the public debts of other countries, or to invest more public funds in them, or to reform the rules of international organizations to which they belong. And the most powerful governments, such as that of the United States, bear greater responsibility than others. The point is that people must do the difficult, mature, adult work of gaining clarity about the kind of responsibility they exercise in specific institutions and organizations. Otherwise, talk of changing the world quickly loses its force because the words dissipate in a shapeless void.

For example, it may be possible to inspire one person or a group of Christians to take action by investing in a microenterprise development organization such as Opportunity International. But acting in that way is very different from exercising influence in or on the World Bank or the United States government. Those who think of Christian responsibility too narrowly in individual or small-group terms will not be able to escape a sense of powerlessness in the larger public world in which they live and work.

If Goudzwaard and those responding to him have delivered a wake-up call, they have done so by calling our attention to the fact that the daily circumstances of our world that we witness on television's evening news do not just happen as a fate outside our responsibility. Moreover, we cannot read the foregoing essays without becoming conscious that the true God and competing idols are warring for our souls and for our entire lives. Economic activity is not a neutral secular affair. The extremes of wealth and poverty in the world are not just interesting facts. And they certainly are not inevitable. Christians who relate to Jesus only as their personal Savior, only as Lord of the church, and only as King in heaven need to be fully converted to realize that God through Christ Jesus is judging and reconciling the whole world. And among the important arenas of this world, which God governs, are the institutions and cultural patterns of economic and political life for which humans bear different kinds of real responsibility.

This, it seems to me, is where the value of the *maturation* metaphor is most useful. Children not only depend on adults, they take for granted the shape of the world in which they grow up. Theirs is a world made up largely of small responsibilities that one child can do or that one child can gradually learn to do with several other children, with a teacher, with siblings, and with parents. Unfortunately, too many adult Christians continue to think in a childish fashion about their *Christian* responsibility in this world: They think chiefly of the deeds they can perform individually or in small groups. They do this because they think too narrowly of their responsibility to Christ as a person-to-person responsibility, such as that of brother to brother, sister to sister, child to parent, wife to husband, husband to wife, and friend to friend. The Bible, however, reveals Jesus Christ to be much more than this. Jesus the bridegroom, the elder brother, and friend is also Head of the whole church, King of Kings, Judge of the living and the dead, Administrator of God's global *oikonomia,* and Master of the seas, the winds, and of the largest human institutions.

In order to serve this Lord, we must respond with an awareness that God calls us to more than individual responsibility in a world that is otherwise a mechanism or a fate beyond our control. We must learn how *we*—not just *I*—should shape business enterprises, government policies, and banking systems. *We* must grow up to realize that *institutions* and *organizations* bear real responsibilities before God in this world. And those responsibilities are exercised by institutional officeholders. Most of the important economic, political, and technological decisions in the world today are made by authorized bodies of people: members of legislatures, boards of directors, corporate managers, international organization heads.

Moreover, in these larger, public institutions, Christians and non-Christians typically *share* responsibility—as citizens or government officials in the same country, as employees or board members of the same corporation, as stockholders or managers in the same company. This is one reason why Goudzwaard can see the possibility of constructive change being fostered by non-Christians and can call for governments and transnational corporations to reform their policies. The reason is *not* because he assumes that all the people in these organizations have undergone conversion to Jesus Christ, but because God's grace in upholding and redeeming the world influences everyone and calls everyone to account, even those who do not acknowledge the true God. God's Spirit is at work throughout the world and is not dependent on Christians alone to convey divine grace. At the same time, Christians, who have been converted to God in Christ, often still exhibit their old, fallen nature. Sometimes they keep holding on to errors, especially negative cultural patterns and institutional structures, that ought to have been reformed long ago.

Part of growing to maturity means recognizing that what is right and just and stewardly holds officials accountable in different institutions even if they do not acknowledge the deepest reason why. Part of leaving childhood behind means learning to accept what God taught Joseph and Daniel, namely, that they were called to serve God in high government posts in Egypt and Babylon for the good of both Israel and of Israel's captors. Part of growing up means learning to work for justice, good stewardship, and the socioeconomic well-being of all our neighbors through common, public institutions in which leaders may bring about healthy and wise changes even if they and the wider culture have not undergone conversion. Part of growing up means learning to take all of God's creation seriously and to exercise responsibility in institutions and organizations of which we are a part by seeking reform in accord with creation-order standards that the Creator has ordained.

Brian Fikkert and Larry Reed are correct that Christians can make a genuinely reforming difference through a Christian microenterprise development organization, through their churches, in their families, in other Christian organizations, and in their own investment patterns. But Christians ought also to seek reforms in major public institutions, reforms of the kind that go beyond accommodation to the fact of parochial self-interest. In some cases, the possibility of devising and accomplishing such reforms will depend heavily on the prior work of Christian schools and colleges, Christian political organizations, and associations of Christian business people, attorneys, or medical professionals. The aim of these kinds of Christian organizations, however, should be to discern and propose normative reforms for academic work and the practice of government, business, law, and medicine in which both Christians and non-Christians are bound together in God's one creation order.

Goudzwaard's reference early in his essay to "selective normative criteria" and Fikkert's and García de la Sienra's references to Kuyper's understanding of sphere sovereignty are especially relevant here. Discerning what constitutes obedience to God means discerning criteria that are appropriate to different kinds of institutions and human responsibilities. Economically speaking, Goudzwaard wants to encourage the growth of "full-blossoming" economies rather than merely economic "expansion" along one track of development. All of this requires careful judgments about the interrelationship of different kinds of enterprise, stewardship, social relationships, and more.

In sum, we might say that the wake-up call we all need to hear today—Christians as well as non-Christians—is that the direction globalization is taking is not inevitable, and it is not all good or all bad. To achieve significant change that addresses world poverty, that can halt and even reverse environmental degradation, and that can point human beings in a full-blossoming direction, it is necessary for those who bear actual responsibility for specific institutions to make important decisions appropriate to those institutions. Many changes for the good will, by God's grace, be made by people of different faiths, and many changes for the worse, toward even greater evil, will also be made by the same people. This is why Christians must recognize that a religiously deep conversion of peoples and cultures is needed to fuel principled, long-term, ongoing transformation of society and the world. But Christians should neither wait for society-wide conversion of individuals before they seek and bear witness to the structural reforms that are needed in society, nor should they expect that social reforms, even when obedient to God, will of themselves assure the renewal of all of society down to the religious roots of human life.[1]

Global Actors

Goudzwaard affirms the legitimacy of globalization, rightly unfolded. What is needed are selective normative criteria for promoting healthy development and resisting unhealthy patterns of globalization. At the religious root, people need conversion from an evolutionary, survival-of-the-fittest worldview that fosters a narrow, "expansionist" quest for more and more wealth. The good news that people need to hear and believe is that God's *oikonomia* in Christ restores good stewardship oriented toward the survival of the weakest and the nurturing of "full-blossoming" growth that benefits everyone.

In the private and voluntary sector, Goudzwaard, Fikkert, and Reed have given examples of how good stewardship can be encouraged. Establishing criteria for designating "Publicly Authorized Companies," publishing a "Market Efficiency Audit," or grading the social responsibility of companies are means of measuring and applauding the positive practices of companies. The well-being of workers and consumers, the health of the environment and of society can be taken into account in these ways and lifted up for the broader public to see. Reed and Fikkert have emphasized the importance of microenterprise development as another means of redirecting some private investments and energy in a direction not yet taken by major businesses and banks in the less-developed world. And García de la Sierra calls Christian economists to develop a better theory based on the assumption that humans are morally responsive agents and not autonomous individuals.

The larger difficulty seems to come in trying to understand what the major public institutions—governments, transnational corporations, the World Bank and International Monetary Fund, and the World Trade Organization—should do to foster full-blossoming development. Here is where we especially need to think in terms of maturation from childishness to adulthood in assessing multiple institutional responsibilities. One of the reasons why we should not demonize the World Bank, for example, is that some of its early efforts to foster development in poorer parts of the world were not misdirected simply because its decisions were grounded in an idolatrous faith in human autonomy and in economic expansion. Its programs were partially misdirected because of a lack of experience, an immaturity in trying to replicate patterns of growth that had seemed to work in the West. In recent years, as Fikkert points out, the World Bank has matured to the point at which it recognizes some of its earlier errors and is reorienting its programs to encourage sustainable growth that will help the poor and not just the elite of poorer countries. There is today, moreover, the recognition by Western governments that direct aid to countries ruled by highly corrupt governments will likely prove to be counterproductive.

Thus, just as Goudzwaard points to signs of progress such as the Shell company rewriting its corporate code after extended discussions with Dutch church leaders, so we can say that there are signs of maturation at the governmental and international governmental levels where responsible officials are learning more about what does and what does not work in God's creation. Rather than looking for demons and angels, therefore, Christians should be among those who are vigorous in discerning and advocating wise patterns of economic and social development and of sound governance. Proposals need not wait until a majority of individuals have awakened from their hypnosis or until the whole world has been converted to Christ. Some or many of those who bear responsibility for major economic investments and for governance decisions may be ready to act in new and wise ways simply because of the force of circumstances.

This is especially important as we come to recognize the ever increasing need for transnational governance.[2] Many Christians, especially in the United States, hold to an ideology of American nationalism even more strongly than they do to an ideology of earthly happiness through continual economic expansion. The very idea of political authority gravitating from the sovereign U.S. government to international or transnational institutions is anathema. Yet Americans have been among those most committed to worldwide economic development, free trade, the growth of multinational corporations, and global market freedom. One of the consequences of these developments, however, is such a degree of growth in international commerce (including now in intellectual property) and environmental degradation that national governments are less and less able to govern these matters by themselves or by trying to work in tandem. Just as colonial interdependence in early America led to the need for a federal government, and just as economic integration in Europe today is pushing members of the European Community toward federal governance structures, so the growing interdependence of all countries around the globe requires better and stronger transnational as well as international governance structures.

Another comment about maturation is important here. Seeking one's self-interest, or one's corporate interest, or a state's national interest is often interpreted as a selfish defect that needs to be overcome or that must be accommodated as a matter of realism. However, an important distinction must be made between proper self-regard and self-care and the negative disposition of selfishness and mere self-aggrandizement. The biblical command to love one's neighbor as oneself presupposes the legitimacy of self-love. Of course, we may not turn the admonition around and say that self-love is all that each person needs to nurture because it will automatically lead to what is good for one's neighbor. No, we are supposed to genuinely love our neighbors and to do so sacrificially at times. Applying this at the institutional level, we can say that there is nothing evil or wrong about a company looking after its own development and well-being. The owners and managers of a company are not responsible for other companies but for their own. There is nothing wrong with parents giving themselves to the care and love of their own children. It would be a failure of responsibility for them to spend so much time looking after the neighbor's children that they neglected their own. There is nothing wrong with the government of one state giving its attention to the just governance, protection, and enhancement of the people and territory under its authority rather than to the people in other countries.

Precisely at this point, however, is where other levels of institutional and communal responsibility must be taken into account. Individuals are never self-enclosed atoms. Parents are not closed off from everyone other than their own children. Corporate owners, managers, and workers work in a larger environment of political and market conditions and regulations that affect all of society. Those of us who are parents, workers, and employers are also neighbors and citizens. While it is correct that people in their role as parents ought not to be expected to raise all the neighbors' children, and while one corporation should not be asked to protect the natural environment for every other company, it is true, nonetheless, that parents and corporation members and citizens in each country also share the same globe, the same limited natural resources, the same humanity.

What we need internationally, therefore, is not for states to quit being states or for corporations to quit being corporations (though all kinds of reforms in both institutions may be necessary). What we need is for people who bear these responsibilities to realize that they also live in an increasingly interdependent global village that requires additional, transnational institutions and reformed international institutions to help make possible the flourishing of life for all. Proper self-interest, neighborly care, and stewardship must be broadened to comprehend global self-care, neighborly care, and stewardship. It is possible, of course, that many states, like the United States, and many corporations may selfishly prefer to subordinate all other concerns and obligations to their own perceived interests narrowly conceived. They may prefer to suffer decline, bankruptcy, and even disintegration rather than open themselves to trans-corporate, transnational norms and governance structures needed for healthy globalization. But the fault in that case would not be because they pursued legitimate self-interest but because of their insistence on remaining captive to the belief that the only way their interests could be pursued was independently, autonomously, and without regard to the needs of other states or corporations and the global conditions for the well-being of all. The answer to worldwide needs will not be found by either demonizing or worshiping self-interest. Instead, we should recognize the limits of self-care and self-regard that properly belong to any individual, family, corporation, or state and then respect and relativize those legitimate concerns in the light of additional levels of human obligation that require still other kinds of institutional actors and responsibilities.

What Must Be Done?

The difficulty of knowing how to create a more just and equitable world is demonstrated in the preceding essays. Goudzwaard calls for awakening, maturation, and conversion to a new way of life that will make possible the survival of the weakest. His appeal culminates in a five-step admonition: (1) that people should, as adults, learn to be satisfied with enough and give up the childish desire always to have more; (2) that people should learn self-restraint, including restraint of wage increases, out of regard for those in greater need; (3) that Western economies should become more "blossoming" instead of merely "expansive" in their approaches to economic growth, and that this will require governmental efforts to preserve the environment, fight world hunger, and promote meaningful employment, better health care, and educational opportunity even when such actions do not maximize financial returns; (4) that people should work to overcome the impersonal anonymity of the larger corporate/political world by taking steps to see the face of the other and to recognize "publicly authorized companies"; and (5) that governments in particular should (a) work to protect the weak by regulating global finance so it is more strongly tied to the real economy and so that the poorest countries can get a new, debt-free start on development and gain greater access to capital; (b) gain greater control over information technology networks to "prevent the subjugation of human consciousness to the expanding control of private commercial interests"; and (c) do more to protect the world's ecosystem especially out of regard for future generations.

Keeping in mind that Goudzwaard did not intend in this lecture to develop concrete proposals to present to the World Bank, or to the U.S. and Dutch governments, or to the European Union, his admonition is, nonetheless, strong on advocating a new spirit and orientation in people generally while being weak in specifying which institution bears responsibility for what kind of action. Even with regard to his recommendations for government action, many of his admonitions focus on a needed outcome more than on the policies that one institution or another ought to adopt. And since many of his aims for global justice will require multinational/international cooperation among governments and probably stronger transnational governing institutions, it is unclear how much can be achieved within the present international institutional framework. Clearly, therefore, organizations such as the Center for Public Justice, which want to develop public policy recommendations and proposals, face a great deal of work in order to understand what and how much the current states and corporations can do and how much of what ought to be done will require new or reformed international and transnational institutions.

Fikkert is cautious about efforts that aim to promote global justice and emphasizes the importance of dealing realistically with the self-interest of states, as was done in setting up the General Agreements on Tariffs and Trade (GATT). He is correct to raise questions about debt forgiveness to the poorest countries unless the terms of that forgiveness can assure those countries of future investments under reformed conditions. Since the debts incurred did not, at the time, presuppose the biblical Jubilee laws, there was no preestablished framework for future release from debt in seven or fifty years. Thus, the reform of the international finance system is as important as, if not more important than, forgiving the current debt of the poorest countries. This is also what Goudzwaard has in mind. But precisely what the new arrangement should be and what changes it would require in the policies of the International Monetary Fund, the World Bank, and various national governments is not clear. Fikkert applauds what he sees as constructive changes in World Bank policies toward poor countries, and he stresses the multi-institutional, holistic approach that is needed to overcome poverty. But again, most questions about which institution (old or new, national or transnational) ought to do what to bring about greater global justice are left unanswered.

Reed focuses on personal responsibility and on the hypothetical difference millions of Christians throughout the world could make. He challenges Christians in particular to voluntarily act with greater restraint in their consumption patterns and with more regard to others in their investment and stewardship patterns. He, like Goudzwaard, also supports the idea of calling attention to responsible companies through different auditing measures. At the corporate, governmental, and international levels he supports changes in the way the IMF and the U.S. Treasury deal with poor countries, as well as for a cautious and reformist approach to debt relief for the most indebted poor countries. The changes he would support are not specified, however.

Finally, García de la Sienra takes up Goudzwaard's specific challenge to overcome mechanistic thinking about economic life and urges economists to develop a theory that accounts for the fact that humans are neither autonomous individuals nor merely conditioned animals but respond to moral norms of a diversified nature. The implications of this approach are extensive, but the immediate appeal is largely to Christian economists to respond voluntarily to the challenge. What all of this might mean for changing the policy decisions of major international institutional actors or for developing new institutions is not clear.

In sum, the preceding essays urge us to wake up from our passive slumbers insofar as we have been hypnotized into believing that there is nothing we can do but to go along with the current trends in globalization. These essays also challenge us, most importantly, to realize that the root of change is religiously deep, not just for individuals but for cultures and societies. The forces driving economic, technological, and political development forward are not surface patterns. The true God of heaven and earth is contending with the false gods that we in our sinfulness choose to serve instead. The challenge of these essays that most needs further elaboration is the one about leaving childishness behind and becoming responsible adults in obedience to the true God. The decision to accept—and the ability to bear—adult responsibility requires more than a right attitude and intention. It requires action of specific kinds in institutions that bear (or should bear) specific kinds of responsibility. Here is where the most difficult and complex questions of global justice have to be taken up in detail and with great care. What, after all, is good and right and healthy about the contemporary international economic order, about the direction that the World Bank, IMF, and WTO are taking, and about the decisions Western governments are taking in regard to economic, political, and social development both internally and in the poorest parts of the world? What are the bad and wrong and unhealthy characteristics of globalization and the direction it is now taking? How much of what is wrong is due to religious misdirection, and how much of it is due to immaturity of people and institutions in dealing with rapid global changes? What new policies should the world's most influential institutions be adopting, and what new institutions are needed in order for certain kinds of action to be taken?

These questions constitute a major challenge for public officials, corporate leaders, public policy think tanks, and academic economists, political scientists, and sociologists, among others. Christians in all of these positions bear a special responsibility to seek out ways to work together in order to deepen their Christian worldview and to develop the implications of that worldview for a just international economic order. This is also part of what growing up and maturing means for Christians. At this point in history, with millions of Christians worldwide able to communicate with one another more and more easily in a diverse array of academic, economic, ecclesiastical, professional, social service, and political organizations, we fail to honor Christ if we do not work together more vigorously to understand and help shape globalization in obedience to God's creation-order norms. We must extend ourselves beyond missions and voluntary service and become adults, as Hebrews 5:11–6:3 urges, in order to understand and practice righteousness. Righteousness (justice) means discerning carefully in every detail of our creaturely responsibilities the difference between good and evil in order to promote the good. And this can be done in our rapidly differentiating and shrinking world only by learning how to answer the question, Who (which person or institution) bears what kind of responsibility to do what, and how should each one exercise that responsibility in obedient response to God for everyone's good, including the good of our neighbors who stand in the greatest need?

Notes

Foreword

1. Alan Cowell, "What Can the New Economy Do for Places without an Old One?" *New York Times,* 23 April 2000.

Chapter 1: The Spirit of Our Age

1. Kuyper's 1899 lecture, "Evolutie," has recently been published in English translation in James D. Bratt, ed., *Abraham Kuyper, A Centennial Reader* (Grand Rapids: Eerdmans, 1998), 405–40.

2. Ibid., 414.

3. Ibid.

4. Ibid., 409.

5. Ibid., 408.

6. Bernard Zylstra, "The Kingdom of God: Its Foundations and Implications," in *Confessing Christ in Doing Politics: Essays on Christian Political Thought and Action,* ed. B. J. van der Walt and R. Swanepoel (Potchefstroom, South Africa: Institute for Reformational Studies, University of Potchefstroom, 1995), 25–46.

7. Harvey Cox, "The Market as God," *The Atlantic Monthly* (March 1999), 20.

8. See Jacques Ellul, *The Technological Society,* trans. John Wilkinson (New York: Vintage Books, 1964).

9. David Korten, *When Corporations Rule the World* (San Francisco: Berret-Koehler, 1995).

10. For a summary, see John B. Judis, "Summer's Day: Should an Economist Be in Charge of the Economy?" *The New Republic* (7 June 1999), 20–24; and Paul Krugman, "Recovery? Don't Bet On It," *Time* (21 June 1999), 76–81.

11. Carl Shapiro and Hal Varian, *Information Rules: A Strategic Guide to the Network Economy* (Berkeley: University of California Press, 1999).

Chapter 2: An Assessment of Globalization

1. The opposite view is also sometimes defended: Every "free" economic and technological development is applauded as a step toward the coming of the kingdom. Michael Novak gives this impression, for example, when he speaks of the modern business corporation as "a much despised incarnation of God's presence in this world." See Michael Novak, "Toward a Theology of the Corporation," in *On Moral Business: Classical and Contemporary Resources for Ethics in Economic Life,* ed. Max L. Stackhouse, Dennis P. McCann, and Shirley J. Roels (Grand Rapids: Eerdmans, 1995), 775.

2. See, for example, Marilynne Robinson's attempt to recover Calvin from misunderstanding in her *The Death of Adam: Essays on Modern Thought* (Boston: Houghton Mifflin, 1998), especially 174–226.

3. This is similar to what Dietrich Bonhoeffer understood by living in the penultimate time *(das Vor-letzte).*

4. In his day, in a similar context, Abraham Kuyper criticized the drive toward uniformity as "the curse of modern life" (Bratt, *Abraham Kuyper,* 19).

5. George Soros, *The Crisis of Global Capitalism: Open Society Endangered* (New York: Perseus Books Group, 1998).

6. George Soros and Jeff Madrick, "The International Crisis: An Interview," *The New York Review of Books* (14 January 1999). Soros adds here, "The need is to find a mechanism to provide capital to the periphery when the market will not do so" (38).

7. Ibid.

8. Dietrich Bonhoeffer, *Christology* (London: Collins, 1966); quoted in Peter Selby, *Grace and Mortgage: The Language of Faith and the Debt of the World* (London: Darton, Longman and Todd, 1997), 16. Bonhoeffer adds here, "'How are you possible?'—that is the godless question, the serpent's question."

9. Johan Witteveen, "Economic Globalisation in a Broader, Long-Term Perspective: Some Serious Concerns," in *The Policy Challenges of Global Financial Integration*, ed. Jan Joost Teunissen (The Hague: Fondad, 1998), 17–33.

Chapter 3: Structural and Cultural Dimensions of Globalization

1. See, for example, William Greider, *One World, Ready or Not: The Manic Logic of Global Capitalism* (New York: Simon and Schuster, 1997); John Gray, *False Dawn* (London: Granta Books, 1998); George Soros, *The Crisis of Global Capitalism: Open Society Endangered* (New York: BBS/PublicAffairs, 1998).

2. One of the most widely read economic books of our time is Michael E. Porter's *The Competitive Advantage of Nations* (New York: Free Press, 1990). Manuel Castells's description of the new global economy is similar: "Productivity and competitiveness are the commanding processes of the informational/global economy." *The Information Age*, vol. 3, *End of the Millennium* (Oxford: Blackwell, 1998), 355. Compare this with the title of Paul Krugman's famous article, "Competitiveness, a Dangerous Obsession," *Foreign Affairs* (spring 1994): 28–44.

3. Dan Schiller, "Bataille mondiale pour le controle des reseaux," in *Revolution dan la Communication*, a special edition of *Le Monde Diplomatique* (July–August, 1999): 12.

4. Benjamin R. Barber, "Culture McWorld contre democratie," *Le Monde Diplomatique* (July–August 1999): 73 (my translation).

5. Joseph S. Nye and Admiral William A. Owens, *Foreign Affairs* (March 1996); quoted in ibid., 67.

6. On the distinction between affirmation and self-affirmation, see A. A. A. Terruwe and C. Baars, *Loving and Curing the Neurotic: A New Look at Emotional Illness* (New Rochelle, N.Y.: Arlington House, 1972).

7. "Accelerated Climate Change: Sign of Peril, Test of Faith," a study paper from the World Council of Churches, Geneva, May 1994.

8. Manuel Castells stated this recently as follows: "Under the information paradigm, a new culture has emerged: *the culture of real virtuality* [his italics]. . . . I mean a system in which reality itself is fully immersed in a virtual image setting, in the world of make believe, in which symbols . . . comprise the actual experience" (*Information Age*, 350).

9. The well-known report of the Group of Lisbon, *Limits to Competition* (Cambridge: The MIT Press, 1995), speaks about an ideology that is centered in the dogma or credo of competitiveness: "Industrialists, politicians, economists, financial leaders, technologists and trade unionists have adopted the competitiveness metaphor as their credo" (91–93).

10. From Friedrich Nietzsche's "The Gay Science" *(Die froehliche Wissenschaft)*, excerpted in Walter Kaufmann, ed., *Existentialism from Dostoevsky to Sartre* (New York: Meridian Books, 1956), 104–7. Richard Wagner, the great composer, was inspired by Nietzsche and, not by accident, was also the first composer to use the free-floating scale because he rejected the idea of a given base within one piece of music. Cows usually refuse to give milk when the music of Wagner is played instead of the music of Bach or Beethoven. Perhaps there is an analogy between these stories and what will happen in the world of finance.

Chapter 4: Breaking Free from the Hypnosis of Our Age

1. TINA has become the slogan of both the transnational Shell corporation and the World Trade Organization.

2. It seems that Kuyper foresaw something of this. In speaking about the final consequences of modernity, he predicted that "man [would] yield himself to the mystical current of an endless process, a *regressus* and *processus in infinitum*." From Kuyper's 1898 Stone Lectures at Princeton University, in *The Crown of Christian Heritage*, introduced by Vishal Mangalwadi (Landour, India: Nivedit Good Books Distributors, 1994), 154.

3. C. S. Lewis, *Till We Have Faces* (Grand Rapids: Eerdmans, 1956).

4. Eberhard Bethge, *Bonhoeffer: Exile and Martyr* (London: Collins, 1975), 129–42.

5. Friedrich Weinreb, *Ik die verborgen ben* (The Hague, Netherlands: Servire, n.d.), 45.

6. Compare this with what the Russian Christian philosopher Nicolai Berdyaev (1874–1948) once wrote: "Both Capitalism and Socialism developed on the basis of a spiritual decline, as the result of a long process of denial of the spiritual center of life, namely God. . . . To go on living, the deprived peoples should perhaps go a different way, namely the way of a restriction of an unreasonable (excessive) growth of their material needs and of the size of their own populations—the way of a new asceticism." *Das neue Mittelalter* [The New Middle Ages] (Tubingen: Otto Reichl Verlag, n.d.), 39 (my translation).

7. See Stephan Schmidheiny, ed., with the Business Council for Sustainable Development, *Changing Course: A Global Business Perspective on Development and the Environment* (Cambridge: The MIT Press, 1992).

8. The report of these meetings is only available in Dutch: *Shell en de Raad van Kerken in Gesprek* (Driebergen: Kerk en Wereld, 1998).

9. See George Goyder, *The Responsible Company* (Oxford: Blackwell, 1961); and *The Responsible Worker* (London: Hutchinson, 1976).

Response by Brian Fikkert

1. World Bank, *World Development Report* (1999), iii.

2. For a helpful review, see Craig M. Gay, *With Liberty and Justice for Whom? The Recent Evangelical Debate Over Capitalism* (Grand Rapids: Eerdmans, 1991).

3. A closely related school of thought, which many Christians find appealing, is the Austrian school of economics. Like the neoclassical school, it emphasizes the value of individuals being given the liberty to pursue free exchange without hindrances from the government. The Austrian and neoclassical schools differ in that

the latter believes that in some situations the government may actually be able to overcome "market failures" in which potentially, mutually beneficial exchanges fail to occur. In contrast, the Austrian school believes that the government never has as much information as the private sector, making it impossible for the government to improve upon whatever the free market has achieved. In this sense, the Austrian school is more libertarian than the neoclassical school. However, both systems share the implicit ethical standard that autonomous individuals are the proper reference point for determining the allocation of society's resources.

4. One could give similar critiques of the presuppositions behind socialism, but I have chosen to focus on laissez-faire capitalism because it is this system that has lulled the West to sleep.

5. Ken Elzinga, "A Christian View of the Economic Order," *Reformed Journal* (October 1981): 16.

Response by Larry Reed

1. Ron Sider, "Take the Pledge: A Practical Strategy for Loving the Poor," *Christianity Today* (7 September 1998), 84.

2. Evans Maphenduka and Larry Reed, "Holistic Lending at Zambuko Trust," in *Serving with the Poor in Africa,* ed. Yamamori et al. (Monrovia, Calif.: MARC, 1996), 67–78.

3. MicroCredit Summit Campaign, www.microcreditsummit.org

4. World Bank, www.worldbank.org/poverty/data/trends/income.htm.

5. Susan Powell, "The Master's Joy," *Re:Generation* (January 1999).

6. Sider, "Take the Pledge," 84. At first glance this number may seem difficult to believe, but when you consider that people who declare themselves to be Christians make up two billion of the world's six billion people, it does not seem unreasonable that they would earn one quarter of the world's income. If anything, this number may underestimate their earnings.

7. World Bank, *Development Report* (1999).

8. 1999 Fortune Global 500, *Fortune* magazine.

9. World Bank, *Development Report* (1999).

10. Walt Kelly, Pogo cartoon, Earth Day 1971.

11. Gunther Risse, *Mending Bodies, Saving Souls* (New York: Oxford University Press, 1999).

12. Oral History of Dame Cicely Saunders, Louise M. Darling Biomedical Library, UCLA.

13. Rodney Clapp, "Why the Devil Takes VISA," *Christianity Today* (7 October 1996), 18.

14. Joe Musser, *The Cereal Tycoon* (Chicago: Moody Press, 1997).

15. Hamish Pringle and Marjorie Thompson, *Brand Spirit* (New York: John Wiley and Sons, 1999).

16. David Dorsey, "The New Spirit of Work," *Fast Company* (August 1998), 124.

17. Quoted in Sustainable Seattle, www.scn.org.

18. David Korten, "The Responsibility of Business to the Whole," People-Centered Development Forum, 20 May 1997.

19. Council for Economic Priorities, www.cepnyc.com. Their seven categories are environment, women's advancement, minority advancement, charitable giving, workplace issues, family benefits, and disclosure.

20. Simon Zadek and Richard Evans, "Auditing the Market—a Practical Guide to Social Auditing," *Tradecraft Exchange* (1993).

21. Janet Atkinson-Grosjean, "On Higher Ground," *CGA Magazine* (May 1999).

22. Clapp, "Why the Devil Takes VISA," 18.

23. The Social Investment Forum (www.socialinvest.org) provides a list of social investment mutual funds and assistance in analyzing the holdings of mutual funds.

24. Dorsey, "The New Spirit of Work," 124.

25. Paul Johnson, *A History of Christianity* (New York: Penguin Books, 1976).

26. Obituary, *Economist* (31 December 1999).

27. Jan Nattier, "Why Buddhism? Why Now?" *Civilization* (January 2000).

Response by Adolfo García de la Sierra

1. For a study of the scholastic doctrines and their replacement by the modern ones, see Francisco Gomez Camacho, *Economica y filosofia moral* (Madrid: Sintesis, 1998).

2. This was done in a very conscious and deliberate way during the nineteenth century. See Philip Mirowski, *More Heat than Light: Economics as Social Physics, Physics as Nature's Economics* (Cambridge: Cambridge University Press, 1989).

3. George Soros, *La crisis del capitalismo global* (Madrid: Plaza Janes, 1999), 62.

4. Ibid., 241.

5. Kenneth Arrow, *Social Choice and Individual Values* (New Haven: Yale University Press, 1963).

6. Ibid., 17.

7. Ibid. For a complete survey of the literature on this theorem until the mid-1980s, see Amartya Sen, "Social Choice Theory," in *Handbook of Mathematical Economics,* vol. 3 (Amsterdam: Elsevier, 1986), 1073–181.

8. Arrow, *Social Choice,* 89.

9. Duncan Black, "On the Rationale of Group Decision Making," *Journal of Political Economy* 56 (1948): 23–34.

10. Arrow, *Social Choice,* 89.

11. See A. Mas-Colell, M. D. Whinston, and J. R. Green, *Microeconomic Theory* (Oxford: Oxford University Press, 1995).

Conclusion by James W. Skillen

1. A number of Christian efforts are under way to study or help shape constructive globalization. "Globalization: A Challenge for Peace" is a research project of the International Jacques Maritain Institute (Rome) that began in 1998. See the report in English in the Institute's periodical *Notes et Documents* (January–August 1999): 42–65. Professor Max Stackhouse of Princeton Theological Seminary is also pursuing research in this area, which is engaging Christians throughout the world. See his article "Mutual Obligation as Covenantal Justice in a Global Era," Zadok Paper #S102 (Zadok Institute for Christianity and Society, Hawthorne, Victoria, Australia, 1999–2000). Also from the Zadok Institute is Bruce Duncan's "Public Theology in a Global Catholic Perspective," *Zadok Perspectives* (autumn 2000): 17–20. Another international Catholic project is unfolding at the Woodstock Theological Center of Georgetown University in Washington, D.C. See the report on

"Global Economy and Cultures" in the *Woodstock Report* (October 1999): 2–8. For an evaluation of some evangelical and Reformed efforts, see Fred Van Geest, "A Reformed Christian Perspective on Global Justice and Political Economy," *Pro Rege* (Dordt College, September 1999): 9–23.

2. See Robert Gilpin, *The Challenge of Global Capitalism* (Princeton: Princeton University Press, 2000), who argues that the global economy is only as strong and as just as its political institutions.

Bob Goudzwaard is professor emeritus, Free University of Amsterdam. He was elected to the Dutch Parliament in the 1970s and served for a time in a Christian policy research institute in The Hague. He now works with a coalition of Dutch churches to address Third World poverty and other aspects of an international Christian witness. His books include *Beyond Poverty and Affluence: Towards an Economy of Care* (Eerdmans, 1995); *Idols of Our Time* (InterVarsity, 1984); and *Capitalism and Progress: A Diagnosis of Western Society* (Eerdmans, 1980).